Arising to Serve

Ruhi Institute

Books in the Series:

Below are the current titles in the series designed by the Ruhi Institute. The books are intended to be used as the main sequence of courses in a systematic effort to enhance the capacity of youth and adults to serve their communities. The Ruhi Institute is also developing a set of courses that branch out from the third book in the series for training teachers of Bahá'í children's classes, as well as another set from Book 5 for raising up animators of junior youth groups. These, too, are indicated in the list below. It should be noted that the list may undergo change as experience in the field advances, and additional titles will be added as a number of curricular elements under development reach the stage where they can be made widely available.

Permission for a limited printing of this book has been granted to Baha'i Books UK by the Ruhi Institute.

Baha'i Books UK
27 Rutland Gate
London
SW7 1PD
books@bahai.org.uk
www.bahaibooks.org.uk

Ruhi Institute
Cali, Colombia
Email: instituto@ruhi.org
Website: www.ruhi.org

Contents

A Few Thoughts for the Tutor

This book, the second in the main sequence of courses offered by the Ruhi Institute, is concerned with capabilities that enable us to contribute to meaningful and uplifting conversation. The specific act of service on which the book focuses is described in the third unit. In a world in which powerful forces are tearing communal bonds asunder, the practice of visiting friends and neighbors in their homes to explore themes central to the life of society can, if it becomes a prominent feature of culture, remedy some of the ills engendered by increasing isolation. The ties of fellowship thus created, the unit suggests, serve to fortify the process of building vibrant and harmonious communities.

A sustained program of visits to homes in a neighborhood or village calls for a degree of organization, involving a nucleus of dedicated friends supported by the requisite administrative institutions and agencies. In guiding a group through the book, the tutor should bear in mind that participants are being prepared to join such an ongoing effort. Visits arranged for them as a component of their study should lead to a commitment to take part in this effort year after year, an important aspect of a life of service.

The practice of visiting homes for the explicit purpose of exploring themes of spiritual and social significance clearly enriches the culture of a community. Equally crucial in this respect are the many informal discussions that occur at home and in the workplace, at school and in the market. To introduce spiritual principles into everyday conversation from time to time, then, is an ability that deserves attention. Its development is the focus of the second unit, laying, in this way, a foundation for the study undertaken in the third.

If our conversations with friends and neighbors are to be uplifting, we must be able to bring joy to our interactions with them. This is the subject addressed in the first unit, "The Joy of Teaching". All the acts of service recommended by the Ruhi Institute involve, in essence, sharing with others the pearls of divine wisdom that we discover in the ocean of Bahá'u'lláh's Revelation. The study of the first unit is intended to heighten awareness of the joy inherent in this pursuit. Participants are asked over several sections to think about the Word of God and what a blessing it is to share it with others. From this act, the unit proposes, arises the joy that quickens our steps as we walk the path of service. Yet, even when fully convinced of this profound spiritual truth, we can lose the joy of teaching if we fail to give thought to the qualities and attitudes that must distinguish service. These are the object of discussion in many subsequent books in the series, and only a few are examined here, beginning with detachment in Section 7. A selection of quotations from the Bahá'í Writings forms the basis for reflection on this quality, a quality indispensable if external factors are not to diminish the joy of service. What is important is that participants not come away from their study with the mistaken notion that detachment implies aloofness or lack of care. We must constantly strive to intensify our exertions and to increase the efficacy of our service as we endeavor to achieve better and better results. This requires an adequate understanding of the character of effort, a topic that is considered in Section 8. Optimism and gratefulness, two attitudes fundamental to the path of service, are briefly discussed in the next and final section.

The second unit of the book, "Uplifting Conversations", focuses on the ability to elevate the level of informal conversation by referring to spiritual principles when occasion permits. It consists of a number of short statements on various subjects, which, though not exact quotations, are based on 'Abdu'l-Bahá's utterances and include many of the words and phrases He used. Of universal appeal, they speak to the aspirations and concerns of people of all backgrounds. It is hoped that, by studying the statements, participants will draw inspiration from the manner in which 'Abdu'l-Bahá explained spiritual principles and will acquire the habit of looking to Him as they strive to discover the pearls that lie in the ocean of Bahá'u'lláh's Revelation, understand the meaning and implications of His Father's teachings, and share them generously with others.

To achieve the aim of the unit, participants should be given the opportunity to go over each statement several times, identify the sequence of thought, and practice saying it until they have so internalized the ideas that they can express them naturally. Some will, at first, basically memorize the statements and repeat them more or less the way they appear in the unit. This is to be expected. As their knowledge of the Faith deepens and their experience grows, they will have access to a much wider range of content and a much richer vocabulary, which will be reflected in their interactions with others. The tutor should recognize that, at this stage, what is being sought is twofold: a measure of ease in explaining the teachings and alignment with 'Abdu'l-Bahá's thought.

After the members of the group learn to present the content of each statement, they move on to another activity in which they are encouraged to correlate the ideas they have studied with issues of concern to their families, friends, and coworkers. To this end, they are asked to think about some of the topics and questions raised in conversation and decide which ones would offer them the possibility of introducing the ideas into a discussion. For a few statements, an example or two are mentioned to illustrate how the spiritual principles enunciated by 'Abdu'l-Bahá shed light on matters that are of concern to people everywhere. This exercise will yield better fruit if, while study of the book is still in progress, the tutor is able to assist each member in choosing one of the statements and a couple of individuals with whom to converse on the ideas it contains. In this way, time can be set aside for participants, when meeting together, to describe to one another the dynamics of the conversations in which they have engaged.

For every statement in the unit, a few passages from the Writings of Bahá'u'lláh are included for memorization. The emphasis the Ruhi Institute places on memorization, already apparent in the first book in the series, becomes more pronounced in Book 2. It is assumed that, by now, participants are conscious of the spiritual nourishment they receive from bringing to mind passages from the Writings time and again. In this book, then, they will reflect further on the effects of the Word of God on the human heart, and in the third unit, as in the second, they will learn to present principles and ideas found in the Writings in their speech and, when appropriate, quote passages directly. To explain the teachings accurately, giving them to others in their pure form, is among the capabilities we all seek to develop as we walk the path of service. That an excellent place to begin is by studying 'Abdu'l-Bahá's explanations and trying to express them in the manner He did is the premise underlying the structure of the second unit.

As indicated above, the third unit, entitled "Deepening Themes", turns to the act of service addressed in this book—that is, to pay visits to friends and neighbors for the explicit purpose of engaging in discussions vital to the life of the community. Three types of conversation are envisioned in the unit and, for each, specific content is suggested. The first type revolves around a series of themes to be explored with the residents of a village or neighborhood in a program of systematic visits. Although the content outlined could well be shared with interested audiences in a variety of ways, the original intention of the themes—to provide the members of a household with the opportunity to deepen their knowledge of the Faith—remains most relevant. The greater share of the unit, then, is given over to this type of conversation.

Yet, the practice of visiting homes has taken on new dimensions in recent years, especially as smaller and smaller geographic units, all the way down to the level of the village and the urban neighborhood, have seen a rise in the number of individuals who can act as tutors, animators of junior youth groups, and children's class teachers. Notably, the practice has shown itself to be essential not only for the purpose of propagating knowledge of the Faith; it is also imperative to the successful unfoldment of the programs for the spiritual empowerment of junior youth and for the spiritual education of children. In this, what has become clear is that regular visits need to be undertaken by animators and teachers to the parents of youngsters in the two programs to discuss the concepts and approaches which give them shape. Such discussions constitute a second type of conversation, which is examined in Sections 14 and 15. The content covered in these sections is far from extensive, for participants will become much more familiar with the two educational programs in future courses. But for them to be aware of the significance of this type of conversation and to accompany teachers of children and animators of junior youth groups on their visits to parents can prove highly fruitful at this early stage.

A third type of conversation envisioned in the unit serves a very special purpose. So many young men and women are looking for avenues through which their ardent desire to contribute to the betterment of the world can find expression. They represent an enormous reservoir of capacity to change society that is waiting, nay, longing to be tapped. A conversation among peers in which they reflect on the opportunities and responsibilities unique to the period of youth, with all its energy and extraordinary potential, can, more often than not, lead to a discussion around service and kindle interest in the work underway in villages and neighborhoods across the globe. Numerous will, in turn, welcome an invitation to join the institute courses as a means of acquiring the capacity to provide spiritual education to rising generations as children's class teachers and animators of junior youth groups. Sections 9 and 10 set out some ideas that can be explored in this type of conversation.

To strengthen the capabilities that enable individuals to initiate and sustain meaningful conversations, the unit must, of course, go beyond suggesting broad themes and the corresponding content. Apart from the ability to articulate ideas with clarity, participants need to develop the requisite attitudes and spiritual qualities. These underlie much of the account that unfolds in the unit, but their importance to the capabilities in question is made explicit in Section 4, where participants think about what kind of sentiments and thoughts should fill our hearts and minds in preparing for a visit, and in Section 5, where they reflect on the quality of humility. The tutor will want to ensure that these sections receive sufficient attention by participants, for, no matter how much knowledge we acquire, no matter how well we can articulate ideas, the effectiveness of our conversations will depend on the qualities and attitudes we bring to them.

It should be noted that the acts of service described in this series of books, though central to the growth and development of a community, are above all elements of a process that seeks to raise individual capacity through study and action. What every tutor should realize is that these acts build on one another, increasing in terms of complexity from book to book. Learning to carry out each act of service effectively proves crucial to the capacity required to perform those that follow. To maintain an ongoing conversation over the course of several visits to a home, as proposed in this book, is clearly more demanding than the activity encouraged in Book 1, that of hosting a regular devotional gathering, whether on one's own or in collaboration with a few others. And it is not difficult to see how, to undertake the more complex acts of service ahead, it will be essential for participants to advance in the capabilities addressed here.

As mentioned in the introductory remarks in Book 1, participants in the institute courses worldwide come from a diversity of backgrounds and, initially, have varying degrees of familiarity with the Bahá'í teachings. By the time they begin this second book, they will have indeed, each and all, embarked on the path of service opened up by the courses. But some differences remain. In the case of youth, for example, unless they have gone through the educational programs for children and junior youth, many of the statements and themes presented in the book will be new to them, and its study will serve as a means for them to deepen their own knowledge of the Faith. The tutor should stand ready in this respect to exhibit the flexibility and creativity necessary to nurture understanding in every member of the group, while making sure that the main objective of the course, to enable participants to engage in meaningful and uplifting conversation, is achieved. What is more, in the thousands of localities where the book is being employed, the community-building process to which the three units seek to contribute is not at the same point of development. Putting into action what is being learned, then, can assume a somewhat different shape from one locality to the next, and this, too, provides an indication of the care and thoroughness with which a tutor must respond to the needs of every member in taking a group through these pages.

The Joy of Teaching

Purpose

To appreciate that the joy of teaching lies
in the act of sharing with others
the Word of God

SECTION 1

Arising to Serve is the second in a sequence of courses offered by the Ruhi Institute that seek to combine study and action. Its aim is to help you advance further along the path of service you have entered as you strive to fulfill a twofold purpose: to pursue your own spiritual and intellectual growth and to contribute to the transformation of society. From your participation in the first course, you must already realize that the path to which we are referring is defined by a series of acts of service, acts that we carry out with our eyes fixed on the goal of a new world order as envisioned in the Writings of Bahá'u'lláh. Thus, much of what we call "walking the path of service" consists of our efforts to apply His teachings to our own lives and to the life of humanity. He Himself speaks of His Revelation in these terms:

> **"O My servants! My holy, My divinely ordained Revelation may be likened unto an ocean in whose depths are concealed innumerable pearls of great price, of surpassing luster. It is the duty of every seeker to bestir himself and strive to attain the shores of this ocean, so that he may, in proportion to the eagerness of his search and the efforts he hath exerted, partake of such benefits as have been preordained in God's irrevocable and hidden Tablets."**[1]

In this first unit, our thoughts turn to the joy that fills our hearts as we discover the pearls of wisdom that lie in the ocean of Bahá'u'lláh's Revelation and share them with others. Already from your study of Book 1 you have seen how exquisitely beautiful are the pearls of divine guidance found in His Writings. Let us ponder on a few excerpts more:

> **"The utterance of God is a lamp, whose light is these words: Ye are the fruits of one tree, and the leaves of one branch."**[2]

> **"The best beloved of all things in My sight is Justice; turn not away therefrom if thou desirest Me, and neglect it not that I may confide in thee."**[3]

> **"Be anxiously concerned with the needs of the age ye live in, and center your deliberations on its exigencies and requirements."**[4]

> **"All men have been created to carry forward an ever-advancing civilization."**[5]

> **"The world passeth away, and that which is everlasting is the love of God."**[6]

> **"Thou art My lamp and My light is in thee. Get thou from it thy radiance and seek none other than Me. For I have created thee rich and have bountifully shed My favor upon thee."**[7]

You may wish to memorize these short passages over time.

SECTION 2

To begin your deliberations on the main theme of this unit, reread the first passage quoted in the previous section and carry out the following exercises:

1. Complete the sentences below.

   a. It is our duty to _____ ourselves and _____ _____ the _____ of the ocean of Bahá'u'lláh's Revelation.

   b. We should strive to attain the shores of the ocean of Bahá'u'lláh's Revelation so that we may partake of such _____ as have been preordained in God's irrevocable and hidden Tablets.

   c. The benefits we partake of the ocean of Bahá'u'lláh's Revelation will be proportional to _____ _____ .

2. What does it mean to "bestir" oneself? _____ _____

3. What does it mean to "strive to attain" something? _____ _____

4. What should every seeker strive to attain? _____ _____

5. What does it mean for one thing to be "in proportion" to another? _____ _____

6. Bahá'u'lláh tells us that we will receive the benefits of the ocean of His Revelation in proportion to the efforts we exert.

   a. Give some examples of the efforts we exert that make us the recipients of these benefits: _____ _____ _____ _____ _____ _____

   b. Give some examples of the benefits we receive: _____ _____ _____ _____ _____ _____

SECTION 3

Knowing that Bahá'u'lláh's Revelation is like an ocean in whose depths lie pearls of inestimable value, we each exert the utmost effort to partake of its benefits and to help others to attain unto its shores. But how far, we may ask ourselves, are the shores of this ocean from us? Bahá'u'lláh declares:

> **"O My servants! The one true God is My witness! This most great, this fathomless and surging Ocean is near, astonishingly near, unto you. Behold it is closer to you than your life-vein! Swift as the twinkling of an eye ye can, if ye but wish it, reach and partake of this imperishable favor, this God-given grace, this incorruptible gift, this most potent and unspeakably glorious bounty."[8]**

1. To what does the phrase "this most great, this fathomless and surging Ocean" refer?

   _____

2. How close is this ocean to us? _____

   _____

3. How quickly can we reach this ocean? _____

   _____

4. Complete the following sentences:

   a. The most great ocean of Bahá'u'lláh's Revelation is near, _____

      _____ , unto us.

   b. The ocean of Bahá'u'lláh's Revelation is _____ to us than our life-vein.

   c. Swift as the _____ we can, if we only wish it,

      _____ and _____ of the ocean of His Revelation.

   d. Swift as the twinkling of an eye we can, _____ ,

      reach and partake of the ocean of His Revelation.

SECTION 4

Having reached the shores of the ocean of Bahá'u'lláh's Revelation, we draw from its treasures and share liberally and unconditionally with others its pearls of divine guidance, which we continually discover in our own study, prayer and meditation and in our efforts to serve His Cause and humanity. You may wish to take some time to memorize the following passage, a constant reminder of the sacredness of this duty:

> **"O wayfarer in the path of God! Take thou thy portion of the ocean of His grace, and deprive not thyself of the things that lie hidden in its depths. Be thou of them that have partaken of its treasures. A dewdrop out of this ocean would, if shed**

upon all that are in the heavens and on the earth, suffice to enrich them with the bounty of God, the Almighty, the All-Knowing, the All-Wise. With the hands of renunciation draw forth from its life-giving waters, and sprinkle therewith all created things, that they may be cleansed from all man-made limitations and may approach the mighty seat of God, this hallowed and resplendent Spot."[9]

SECTION 5

As we advance through the institute courses, carrying out the study and action they require, our capacity for service will grow, and we will be able to undertake acts of service that bring immense joy to our hearts and assist us in fulfilling our twofold purpose—acts such as teaching classes for the spiritual education of children, engaging junior youth in a program for their spiritual empowerment, and helping a group of friends study the books of the main sequence. All throughout this journey, the Word of God, which we will be sharing with others, young and old, will be our constant source of inspiration. It is only proper, then, that we should meditate often on its power and its effect on the human heart. In the following quotation, Bahá'u'lláh speaks of this power:

> **"The Word of God may be likened unto a sapling, whose roots have been implanted in the hearts of men. It is incumbent upon you to foster its growth through the living waters of wisdom, of sanctified and holy words, so that its root may become firmly fixed and its branches may spread out as high as the heavens and beyond."[10]**

1. To what may the Word of God be compared? _____

   _____

2. Where have the roots of the tree of the Word of God been planted? _____

   _____

3. How should we foster the growth of this tree? _____

   _____

4. To what heights can this tree grow? _____

   _____

5. Explain in a few sentences why sharing the Word of God with others is of the utmost importance.

   _____

   _____

   _____

   _____

   _____

SECTION 6

Let us think of the various activities that occupy us in our daily lives. We nourish our bodies. We study to acquire new knowledge and to expand our mental capacity. We work and develop skills that enable us to live as productive members of society. We engage in sports and recreation. Numerous activities like these, all important for our intellectual progress and material well-being, occupy a large portion of our time. But then there are in each day those special moments, charged with spirituality, when we engage in prayer; when we deepen, alone or with friends, our knowledge of divine teachings; or when, in any one of a myriad ways, we help those around us to discover the pearls hidden in the ocean of Bahá'u'lláh's Revelation. Are not these moments precious beyond measure? Is there any greater joy than being able to partake of these heavenly blessings?

We should always remember how 'Abdu'l-Bahá encouraged us to dedicate ourselves to the upliftment of humanity:

> **"We are all united in one Divine purpose, no material motive is ours, and our dearest wish is to spread the Love of God throughout the world!"**[11]

Suppose the opportunity arises for you to share with a friend one of the quotations from Section 1 that you have memorized. Where does the joy you feel in your heart come from? Naturally, you hope your friend will be uplifted by the words of Bahá'u'lláh. But what if he or she does not show the enthusiasm you were expecting? Does the joy in your heart simply vanish? Why not?

_____

_____

_____

_____

_____

SECTION 7

When we realize that, of all the things we do in our lives, the moments we spend sharing the Word of God with others are invested with special blessings, we arrive at a most significant conclusion: that the joy we derive from service lies in the act itself. We hope, of course, that the acts of service we perform will yield worthy results, but if we are too attached to the results, if we are overly affected by praise or criticism, we will lose the joy of teaching. That which should inspire us to serve is the love of God, not the desire to have success, to receive benefits, or to gain recognition. Detachment from all these is a requisite of joyful service. Studying the following quotations will help you reflect on this theme:

> **"O Man of Two Visions! Close one eye and open the other. Close one to the world and all that is therein, and open the other to the hallowed beauty of the Beloved."**[12]

> **"O Friends! Abandon not the everlasting beauty for a beauty that must die, and set not your affections on this mortal world of dust."**[13]

"O Son of Utterance! Turn thy face unto Mine and renounce all save Me; for My sovereignty endureth and My dominion perisheth not. If thou seekest another than Me, yea, if thou searchest the universe forevermore, thy quest will be in vain."[14]

"O Befriended Stranger! The candle of thine heart is lighted by the hand of My power, quench it not with the contrary winds of self and passion. The healer of all thine ills is remembrance of Me, forget it not. Make My love thy treasure and cherish it even as thy very sight and life."[15]

"Detachment is as the sun; in whatsoever heart it doth shine it quencheth the fire of covetousness and self. He whose sight is illumined with the light of understanding will assuredly detach himself from the world and the vanities thereof. . . . Let not the world and its vileness grieve you. Happy is he whom riches fill not with vain-glory, nor poverty with sorrow."[16]

1. Does being detached from this world mean living like a hermit? _____

2. Is it possible to be detached from this world and to possess things at the same time?
   _____

3. Is a person who dedicates practically every hour of life to his or her work detached from the things of this world? _____

4. Is a person who works only enough to satisfy his or her basic needs and spends the rest of the time doing nothing detached from this world? _____

5. Is a person unable to tolerate material discomfort in the field of service detached from the world? _____

6. There are many things to which we can be attached besides material possessions. To what would you be attached if you were a person who

   – wants to give up when he or she performs an act of service and no one acknowledges it? _____

   – feels demoralized when someone does not accept the ideas he or she is sharing?
   _____

   – hides his or her beliefs out of fear of rejection by others? _____
   _____

7. Detachment does not imply aloofness or lack of care. Which of the following could be a sign that one is not detached?

   _____ To derive joy from seeing the progress of others

   _____ To stop teaching a class when a few children misbehave

_____ To brag about one's accomplishments

_____ To study hard and feel content with the progress one makes

_____ To work hard to develop one's capacity to serve the common good

_____ To strive for excellence in one's occupation

_____ To exercise cleanliness and keep a clean and tidy home

_____ To take care of one's belongings

_____ To care for the well-being of others

_____ To be disheartened when not praised for one's efforts

8. So important is detachment for each one of us that it is suggested you memorize all the quotations in this section.

SECTION 8

To receive the bounties of a joyous life of service to humanity, we must be willing to exert effort, and our efforts may require some degree of sacrifice. We use the word "sacrifice" frequently in our daily lives. If a friend is returning from a trip at dawn, we may wake early to pick her up. We may say that we have sacrificed a few hours of sleep. Someone dear to us becomes sick; we forgo a few hours of our favorite pastime to care for him. There are occasions in life when we must work extremely hard, and we may think we are sacrificing comfort in order to meet a goal.

We all have the utmost desire to serve the Cause, generously offering our time and energy and, to the extent possible, a portion of our material resources. When we do so, we should remember that, on the path of service, we may give up things of this world, but what we receive is true joy as we grow spiritually. We will have the opportunity to reflect more on the nature of sacrifice in future courses. What is important to recognize from the very beginning is that it involves renouncing that which is lower for the higher, just as the seed sacrifices itself so a tree can be born. Sacrifice is the bearer of joy, and this joy will not be ours unless we are willing to exert consistent effort.

Bahá'u'lláh states:

"Labor is needed, if we are to seek Him; ardor is needed, if we are to drink the nectar of reunion with Him; and if we taste of this cup, we shall cast away the world."[17]

And 'Abdu'l-Bahá advises us:

". . . rest ye not, seek ye no composure, attach not yourselves to the luxuries of this ephemeral world, free yourselves from every attachment, and strive with heart and soul to become fully established in the Kingdom of God. Gain ye the heavenly treasures. Day by day become ye more illumined. Draw ye nearer and nearer unto the threshold of oneness."[18]

We all believe that, to achieve our goals, we must exert effort. But this simple belief has certain implications in practice that we should not forget. For one, it is necessary to remember that there is a correspondence between the amount of energy required and the level of difficulty of the goal or task at hand. We are deceiving ourselves if we think it can be accomplished with less. But the magnitude of exertion is not the only factor to be taken into account. There is need for consistency and perseverance. Focus is required. The habit of completing tasks, not jumping from one to another and leaving work undone, is essential. Halfhearted efforts do not bear fruit. Imagine a weekly class for the spiritual education of children. The teacher must dedicate a certain number of hours to prepare for each class, remain entirely focused throughout its duration on helping the students understand the content of the lesson, pay regular visits to the parents of the youngsters, and follow their individual progress, week after week. What is the fate of a class whose teacher prepares only occasionally, brings the session to an early and abrupt end when tired, and fails to devote the necessary time to thinking about each child and discussing his or her progress with the parents? And what if the class is simply canceled whenever the teacher wishes to attend to some other obligation, say, to be with a friend who is visiting from out of town?

These few remarks are to convince us that we must give attention to both the amount and the quality of the effort every endeavor we undertake demands. This holds true not only for the acts of service in which we engage; it applies equally to our own development. Even the spiritual habits we considered in the first book of this series—to pray regularly, to read the Writings every day, to ponder how to bring our lives in conformity with the teachings, to participate wholeheartedly in devotional gatherings—depend on continued exertion. Below are a number of statements related to effort. Deciding which ones are true will help you reflect further on this matter:

_____ If you are smart, you don't need to work hard.

_____ Why go the long way; always look for a shortcut.

_____ No pain, no gain.

_____ Dream big; your wishes will come true.

_____ The greater the prize, the greater the striving.

_____ The greater the effort, the sweeter the reward.

_____ If at first you don't succeed, try, try again.

_____ Why work when you can get others to do it for you?

_____ If it takes too much effort, it's not meant to be.

_____ Small steps—frequent and consistent—can go a long way.

_____ Nothing worth having comes easily.

_____ Excellence demands wholehearted dedication.

_____ The journey of a thousand miles begins with a single step.

_____ Just getting by is not good enough.

_____ We should not wait for things to happen; we should pursue them.

_____ Success is a matter of luck.

_____ We won't achieve our twofold purpose by magic.

_____ We must bring ourselves to account each day.

We walk the path of service, striving to achieve our own spiritual and intellectual growth and to contribute to the transformation of society. It is clear that the pursuit of this twofold purpose demands a great deal of effort on our part. Bahá'u'lláh tells us:

> "The incomparable Creator hath created all men from one same substance, and hath exalted their reality above the rest of His creatures. Success or failure, gain or loss, must, therefore, depend upon man's own exertions. The more he striveth, the greater will be his progress."[19]

You may wish to memorize the above passage if you have not already done so.

SECTION 9

To be able to derive joy from service, we should nurture certain attitudes in ourselves. For example, we must be thankful for the bounty of service God has bestowed upon us; it is unthinkable to imagine that we are doing God a favor when we serve His Cause. We must also learn to avoid pessimism and approach life with an optimistic view of the world. Obstacles on the path of service can be turned into stepping-stones to further progress. Even amid difficulties, we look with eyes of faith to the future. The following words of 'Abdu'l-Bahá point to the hope and optimism that should characterize our efforts:

> "In the beginning, how small is the seed, yet in the end it is a mighty tree. Look ye not upon the seed, look ye upon the tree, and its blossoms, and its leaves and its fruits."[20]

> "Know then the vital import of this tiny seed that the true Husbandman hath, with the hands of His mercy, sown in the ploughed fields of the Lord, and watered with the rain of bestowals and bounties and is now nurturing in the heat and light of the Daystar of Truth."[21]

> "When you see a tree growing and developing, be hopeful of its outcome. It will blossom and bear fruit eventually. If you see dry wood or old trees, there is no hope whatever of fruitage."[22]

> "Wherefore must the loved ones of God, laboriously, with the waters of their striving, tend and nourish and foster this tree of hope."[23]

> "If the heart turns away from the blessings God offers how can it hope for happiness? If it does not put its hope and trust in God's Mercy, where can it find rest?"[24]

To reflect on the above passages, complete the following sentences:

1. In the beginning, how small is the seed, yet in the end _____

    _____ .

2.   We should not look at the tiny seed but at _____

_____ .

3.   We should recognize, then, the importance of the tiny seed that God has, with the

hands of His mercy, _____

_____

_____

_____ .

4.   When we see a tree growing and developing, we should be _____

_____ .

5.   When we see a tree growing and developing, we should be hopeful it will _____

_____ .

6.   With the waters of our striving, we should _____

_____ .

7.   If the heart turns away from the blessings God offers _____

_____ ?

8.   If the heart does not put its hope and trust in God's Mercy, _____

_____ ?

Now, reflect for a moment: Do you agree that our joyful and hopeful spirit combined with a posture of humble gratitude is a source of joy to others? And, let us always keep in mind that, in arising to serve the Cause, we bear the glad tidings of the dawn of a new Day, the Day of the ingathering of humankind. May the words of Bahá'u'lláh resound in our hearts:

"Happy are they who act; happy are they who understand; happy the man that hath clung unto the truth, detached from all that is in the heavens and all that is on earth."[25]

REFERENCES

1. *Gleanings from the Writings of Bahá'u'lláh* (Wilmette: Bahá'í Publishing Trust, 1983, 2017 printing), CLIII, par. 5, p. 369.

2. Ibid., CXXXII, par. 3, p. 326.

3. Bahá'u'lláh, *The Hidden Words* (Wilmette: Bahá'í Publishing Trust, 2003, 2012 printing), Arabic no. 2, p. 3.

4. *Gleanings from the Writings of Bahá'u'lláh*, CVI, par. 1, p. 241.

5. Ibid., CIX, par. 2, p. 243.

6. Bahá'u'lláh, in *Women: Extracts from the Writings of Bahá'u'lláh, 'Abdu'l-Bahá, Shoghi Effendi and the Universal House of Justice*, compiled by the Research Department of the Universal House of Justice (Wilmette: Bahá'í Publishing Trust, 1986, 1997 printing), no. 53, p. 26.

7. *The Hidden Words*, Arabic no. 11, p. 6.

8. *Gleanings from the Writings of Bahá'u'lláh*, CLIII, par. 5, p. 370.

9. Ibid., CXXIX, par. 1, p. 316.

10. Ibid., XLIII, par. 9, p. 109.

11. From a talk given on 19 November 1911, published in *Paris Talks: Addresses Given by 'Abdu'l-Bahá in 1911* (Wilmette: Bahá'í Publishing, 2006, 2016 printing), no. 32.2, p. 121.

12. *The Hidden Words*, Persian no. 12, p. 26.

13. Ibid., Persian no. 14, p. 26.

14. Ibid., Arabic no. 15, p. 7.

15. Ibid., Persian no. 32, p. 33.

16. Bahá'u'lláh, in *The Bahá'í World: Volume One, 1925–1926* (Wilmette: Bahá'í Publishing Trust, 1926, 1980 printing), p. 42.

17. *The Call of the Divine Beloved: Selected Mystical Works of Bahá'u'lláh* (Haifa: Bahá'í World Centre, 2018), no. 2.12, p. 17.

18. *Tablets of the Divine Plan: Revealed by 'Abdu'l-Bahá to the North American Bahá'ís* (Wilmette: Bahá'í Publishing Trust, 1993, 2006 printing), no. 13.6, pp. 95–96.

19. *Gleanings from the Writings of Bahá'u'lláh*, XXXIV, par. 8, p. 91.

20.   *Selections from the Writings of 'Abdu'l-Bahá* (Wilmette: Bahá'í Publishing, 2010, 2015 printing), no. 40.3, pp. 118–19.

21.   Ibid., no. 40.3, p. 119.

22.   From a talk given on 11 May 1912, published in *The Promulgation of Universal Peace: Talks Delivered by 'Abdu'l-Bahá during His Visit to the United States and Canada in 1912* (Wilmette: Bahá'í Publishing, 2012), par. 2, p. 153.

23.   *Selections from the Writings of 'Abdu'l-Bahá*, no. 206.13, pp. 356–57.

24.   From a talk given by 'Abdu'l-Bahá on 21 November 1911, published in *Paris Talks*, no. 34.8, p. 133.

25.   Bahá'u'lláh, *Epistle to the Son of the Wolf* (Wilmette: Bahá'í Publishing Trust, 1988, 2016 printing), p. 139.

Uplifting Conversations

Purpose

To acquire the ability to introduce
spiritual principles into a conversation

SECTION 1

In the first unit of this book, we spoke of the immeasurable joy we derive from the act of sharing the Word of God with others. As we walk the path of service, numerous opportunities come to us to discuss with friends and acquaintances the insights we glean from Bahá'u'lláh's Revelation. Among the most essential capabilities we all need to develop, then, are those that enable us to contribute to meaningful and uplifting conversation. The purpose of this unit and the next is to assist you in this respect. Here you will be concerned with how to elevate the level of conversation by referring to spiritual principles, when the occasion calls for it. In the next unit, you will think about how to initiate and sustain a series of conversations on certain themes as part of a systematic effort to build a vibrant community in your village or neighborhood.

What we will do in the sections that follow is to look at a number of statements on various subjects which, though not exact quotations, are all based on talks and Tablets of 'Abdu'l-Bahá and include many of the phrases He used. You should read each statement several times, identify the sequence of ideas, and take turns with the other members of your group saying them aloud until you can express them naturally. This exercise will help prepare you to speak with ease when you find it appropriate to draw on the teachings of the Faith to advance a discussion.

You will continue in this unit, of course, to memorize passages from the Writings, for they have a special power that penetrates the human heart and will, when woven into your speech, have a profound effect on the listener. Yet quoting from the Writings in a conversation requires wisdom. What is necessary is moderation, balance between quoting directly from the Writings and using one's own words to explain the teachings of the Faith. To achieve this balance, you need to devote a great deal of time and energy to the study of the Writings and allow them to shape your thoughts and feelings.

SECTION 2

The first statement you are being asked to study concerns humanity's need for an Educator.

When we consider existence, we observe that the mineral, the vegetable, the animal and the human realms, each and all, are in need of an educator. A garden is in need of a gardener. To yield a plentiful harvest, the land is in need of a farmer. If a man is left alone in the wilderness, he will take on the ways of the animal. If he is educated, he can reach the greatest heights of accomplishment. Were it not for educators, there would be no civilization.

Education is of three kinds: material, human, and spiritual. Material education is concerned with the development of the body. Human education is about civilization and progress. It deals with governance, social order, human welfare, commerce and industry, arts and sciences, momentous discoveries, and great undertakings. Spiritual education consists in acquiring divine perfections. This is true education, for by its aid the spiritual nature, the higher nature, of the human being is developed.

In order to progress, humanity needs an educator who has clear authority as a material, human, and spiritual educator. Should anyone say, "I am endowed with great intelligence, and I have no need for such an educator," he would be denying the obvious. It would be like a child saying, "I have no need of education; I will act according to my own thinking and intelligence and will achieve excellence by myself."

Humanity has always been in need of such a perfect educator, one who can help it organize matters related to the nourishment and health of the body, can inspire it to advance in knowledge, invention and discovery, and, most importantly, can breathe into it the life of the spirit. No ordinary human being is able to achieve these formidable tasks. Only the Manifestations of God have the power to accomplish them. These are chosen Souls Who are sent by God from time to time to be the universal Educators of humanity.

1.   Read the statement several times in your group and help one another learn its content well. You should ask each other questions related to the ideas presented and practice expressing them naturally and with ease.

2.   Next, discuss in your group how the ideas you have learned to articulate here could be introduced into a conversation. Obviously you are not going to all of a sudden say to your friends that education is of three kinds. It is worthwhile, then, for you to think about the types of interactions in which the above ideas would prove relevant. Perhaps the issue under discussion is the moral decline of society or how to work for the betterment of the world. Reflect on the diverse conversations in which you engage with friends, family members, and acquaintances. Among the issues that occupy their minds, are there any which would lend themselves to a discussion around the ideas in this statement?

_____

_____

_____

_____

_____

3.   Questions often arise in conversations on subjects like the one you have just studied. What would you answer if someone asked: "Who are some of these Educators you are talking about?"

_____

_____

_____

4.   Below are a few quotations from the Writings of Bahá'u'lláh related to humanity's need for an Educator. Reflect on them and memorize at least one. In this way, you will be able to weave passages from the Writings into your speech when appropriate.

"All men have been created to carry forward an ever-advancing civilization."[1]

"The Purpose of the one true God, exalted be His glory, in revealing Himself unto men is to lay bare those gems that lie hidden within the mine of their true and inmost selves."[2]

"God's purpose in sending His Prophets unto men is twofold. The first is to liberate the children of men from the darkness of ignorance, and guide them to the light of true understanding. The second is to ensure the peace and tranquility of mankind, and provide all the means by which they can be established."[3]

"Men at all times and under all conditions stand in need of one to exhort them, guide them and to instruct and teach them."[4]

SECTION 3

The following paragraphs describe how God can only be known through His Manifestations and will be helpful to you when conversing with friends:

Consider the infinite universe. Is it possible that it could have been created without a Creator? Or that the reality of the Creator could ever be comprehended by that which He created? If we observe the entire creation, we see that whatever is lower is unable to comprehend the power of that which is higher. So the stone and the tree, however much they may evolve, can never imagine the powers of sight and hearing. The animal can never comprehend the reality of the human being and become aware of the powers of the human spirit. Therefore how can we, the created, understand the reality of our Creator?

Although our understanding can never reach God, we are not deprived of knowing Him. From time to time a special Being appears on earth who is the Manifestation of God. All the perfection, the bounty, and the splendor that belong to God are visible in these Holy Manifestations, like the rays of the sun that appear in a clear, polished mirror. To say that the mirror reflects the sun does not mean that the sun has descended from its heights and become incorporated into the mirror. Likewise, God does not descend from the heaven of sanctity to this plane of existence. What is meant is this: All that humanity knows, learns, and understands of the names and attributes and perfections of God refers to His Holy Manifestations.

1. After reading this statement several times in your group and answering questions posed by one another about its content, you should practice saying the ideas with a measure of ease.

2. Now discuss in your group how you could work into a conversation naturally the ideas you have learned here. This could easily be done, for example, in a discussion about the existence of God or the purpose of life. What are some other topics and questions raised in conversation among your family and friends that would offer you the possibility of sharing these ideas?

_____

_____

_____

_____

_____

3.   Suppose that, in a conversation with your friends, you have an opportunity to introduce the ideas you have just studied. How would you reply if one of them asked you the following question: "What are some of the things we know about God through His Manifestations?"

_____

_____

_____

4.   You may wish to memorize one or more of the following passages from the Writings of Bahá'u'lláh so that you can quote them when you speak with friends on this subject:

"The knowledge of Him, Who is the Origin of all things, and attainment unto Him, are impossible save through knowledge of, and attainment unto, these luminous Beings who proceed from the Sun of Truth."[5]

"The Person of the Manifestation hath ever been the representative and mouthpiece of God. He, in truth, is the Dayspring of God's most excellent Titles, and the Dawning-Place of His exalted Attributes."[6]

"Be ye assured, moreover, that the works and acts of each and every one of these Manifestations of God, nay whatever pertaineth unto them, and whatsoever they may manifest in the future, are all ordained by God, and are a reflection of His Will and Purpose."[7]

SECTION 4

The oneness of religion is a subject of interest to many, and the following ideas will assist you on numerous occasions:

We must be lovers of light no matter from what lamp it appears. We must be lovers of the rose no matter in what garden it blooms. We must be seekers of truth no matter from what source it comes. Attachment to one lamp can prevent us from appreciating the light when it shines in another. In seeking the truth, we must rid ourselves of preconceived notions and give up our prejudices. If our cup is full of self, there is no room in it for the water of life.

Religion is the light of the world. It guides our steps and opens to us the doors of unending happiness. When we investigate the teachings of all the great religions, free from the restrictions of dogmatic beliefs and blind imitation, we come to realize that they rest on the same foundation. They all reveal the knowledge of God. They seek the advancement of the world of humanity.

There are, of course, differences among the social laws and regulations propagated by each religion according to the requirements of time and place. But in their essence all religions are one. They cultivate faith, knowledge, certitude, justice, piety, high-mindedness, trustworthiness, love of God, and charity. They teach purity, detachment, humility, forbearance, patience, and constancy. These human virtues are renewed in every Dispensation.

It is unfortunate that, because of prejudices and blind imitation, many are not able to see the underlying oneness of religion. God's guidance to humanity is truth, and truth has no divisions; it is one. If we investigate the truth independently, setting aside preconceived notions, our search will lead to unity. Religion should unify us; it must establish bonds of love among people. If it becomes the cause of enmity and strife, its absence is preferable.

1. As in the preceding section, you should read this statement several times in your group, ask one another questions related to the ideas, and practice expressing them well.

2. Consider in your group how you might go about weaving the ideas you have studied into a conversation, say, about religious conflict, which is so often on people's minds. But you might also find yourself among several friends discussing the importance of investigating the truth and not being manipulated by propaganda. Think back again to your recent conversations with friends and neighbors, coworkers and acquaintances. What are some issues on their minds that would benefit from a discussion around these ideas?

_____

_____

_____

_____

_____

3. How would you reply if, after sharing the ideas above in conversation, someone asked you, "What are some of the truths common to all religions?"

_____

_____

_____

4. It is suggested that you memorize one or two of the following passages from the Writings of Bahá'u'lláh:

"There can be no doubt whatever that the peoples of the world, of whatever race or religion, derive their inspiration from one heavenly Source, and are the subjects of one God."[8]

"Consort with the followers of all religions in a spirit of friendliness and fellowship."[9]

"The fundamental purpose animating the Faith of God and His Religion is to safeguard the interests and promote the unity of the human race . . ."[10]

"The religion of God is for love and unity; make it not the cause of enmity or dissension."[11]

SECTION 5

The relationship between science and religion is the next subject you are being asked to study.

Religion must be in conformity with science. God has endowed us with reason that we may perceive what is true. Science and religion are both expected to meet the standards of reason. Therefore, they ought to be in agreement with each other. They are the two wings upon which human intelligence can soar to great heights, the two wings with which humanity can fly. One wing is not sufficient.

Science is a bestowal of God. It discovers the laws of the physical world and enables us to overcome the limitations nature has imposed on us. With the aid of scientific instruments, we see things invisible to the naked eye and communicate across vast distances in an instant. Science unites the present and the past and penetrates the mysteries of the future. The progress of a people depends on scientific attainments.

The religion of God is the promoter of truth, the supporter of knowledge, and the civilizer of the human race. Without religion, science becomes a tool to advance materialism, leading eventually to despair. When religion is opposed to science, it becomes mere superstition. If religion and science walk together in harmony, much of the hatred and bitterness now bringing misery to humanity will come to an end.

1.   As always, read the statement several times in your group, paragraph by paragraph, and ask one another questions until you have learned the content well enough to express it naturally.

2.   How would you respond to someone who said the following: "Religion is a thing of the past; science will solve all the problems of humanity." Would it be helpful for you to clarify that religion is not the same as superstition, but it becomes so without science, and that science without religion leads to despair born of materialism? Would you be able to give examples of how this occurs?

_____

_____

_____

_____

_____

3.   It is suggested that you memorize one or more of the following passages from the Writings of Bahá'u'lláh:

"First and foremost among these favors, which the Almighty hath conferred upon man, is the gift of understanding. . . . This gift giveth man the power to discern the truth in all things, leadeth him to that which is right, and helpeth him to discover the secrets of creation."[12]

"Look at the world and ponder a while upon it. It unveileth the book of its own self before thine eyes and revealeth that which the Pen of thy Lord, the Fashioner, the All-Informed, hath inscribed therein."[13]

"Knowledge is as wings to man's life, and a ladder for his ascent. Its acquisition is incumbent upon everyone."[14]

SECTION 6

The oneness of humanity is a subject that resonates in the hearts of people everywhere today, and many will welcome discussing with you the ideas presented below.

A garden in which flowers of many colors and fragrances grow side by side is pleasing to the eye. And though different, each flower is refreshed by the same rain and receives the warmth of one sun. This is also true of humanity. It is made up of many races and colors. But all come from the same God, and all have the same origin. The diversity in the human family should be a source of harmony, as it is in music where different notes blend together to make a perfect chord.

Unity is necessary to existence. Love is the very cause of life. In the material world, the elements of all things are held together by the law of attraction. The law of attraction brings together certain elements in the form of a beautiful flower. But when that attraction is taken away, the flower will decompose and cease to exist. So it is with humanity. Attraction, harmony, and unity are the forces that hold humanity together.

Bahá'u'lláh has made a design for the uniting of all the peoples of the world. We should make every effort to draw them into this circle of unity. When we meet people of races, nationalities, religions, and opinions different than our own, we should not allow these differences to become barriers between us. We should think of them as different colored roses growing in the beautiful garden of humanity and be glad to be among them.

1. After studying the statement above as you did the previous ones, think of the many conversations unfolding around you. What are some of the issues on people's minds that would open up the possibility for you to share these ideas with them?

_____

_____

_____

_____

2.   A conversation on the oneness of humankind may lead to a discussion about the importance of unity in one's own community. Can you say a few words about how each of us can contribute to it?

_____

_____

_____

3.   You may wish to memorize one or more of the following quotations so that you can refer to them when you speak on this subject with your friends:

"The tabernacle of unity hath been raised; regard ye not one another as strangers. Ye are the fruits of one tree, and the leaves of one branch."[15]

"So powerful is the light of unity that it can illuminate the whole earth."[16]

"Set your faces towards unity, and let the radiance of its light shine upon you. Gather ye together, and for the sake of God resolve to root out whatever is the source of contention amongst you."[17]

"It behooveth man to adhere tenaciously unto that which will promote fellowship, kindliness and unity."[18]

SECTION 7

The following statement will help you contribute to discussions on the subject of justice, a matter of great concern to most people:

Difference of capacity in individuals is fundamental to human existence. Therefore, it is not possible for all people to be equal in every respect. Yet human affairs, in their entirety, should be governed by the principle of justice. Justice must be sacred, and the rights of every person must be safeguarded.

Justice is not limited; it is a universal quality. It must operate in all departments of human life. Each and every member of society should enjoy the benefits of civilization, because we all belong to the body of humanity. If one member of this body is in anguish or distress, all the other members inevitably suffer. How can one be afflicted and the others be at ease? Today's society lacks the necessary reciprocity and symmetry; it is not well arranged. Laws and principles are required that will ensure the well-being and happiness of the entire human family.

Justice is established on the pillars of reward and punishment. Governments ruled by those without faith, with no fear of Divine retribution, will execute unjust laws. Hope for reward and fear of punishment are both needed if oppression is to be prevented. Legislators and administrators of the laws must be aware of the spiritual consequences of their decisions. Rulers who believe that the consequences of their actions will follow them beyond this earthly life and who know that their judgments will be weighed in the balance of Divine justice will surely avoid tyranny and oppression.

1. Once you have learned to express the above ideas naturally, consider what topics of conversation would benefit from the insights the statement offers.

_____

_____

_____

_____

2. How would you respond to someone who believes injustice will never end?

_____

_____

_____

3. Below are a few quotations from the Writings of Bahá'u'lláh related to justice that you are encouraged to memorize.

"The light of men is Justice. Quench it not with the contrary winds of oppression and tyranny. The purpose of justice is the appearance of unity among men."[19]

"No radiance can compare with that of justice. The organization of the world and the tranquility of mankind depend upon it."[20]

"That which traineth the world is Justice, for it is upheld by two pillars, reward and punishment. These two pillars are the sources of life to the world."[21]

SECTION 8

The gap between the rich and the poor widens with each passing day, and the statement below will assist you in conversing with friends on this and related subjects.

Today, because of the lack of reciprocity and harmonious relations, some members of society are satisfied, living in great comfort and luxury, while others are in want of food and shelter. Some are enormously rich, and others live in utmost poverty.

The laws of society must be formulated and enforced in such a way that it is not possible for a few to amass inordinate wealth and for others to be destitute. This does not mean that all must be equal, for differences in degree and capacity are inherent to creation. But the deplorable overabundance of wealth accompanied by demoralizing poverty can be abolished. If it be right for a capitalist to possess a fortune, it is equally just that the worker should have a sufficient means of existence. When we see extreme poverty, somewhere we shall find tyranny.

The essence of the matter is that Divine justice must become manifest in human conditions. The fundamentals of the whole economic condition are divine in nature and are associated with the world of the heart and spirit. The rich must give of their abundance; they must soften their hearts and cultivate a compassionate intelligence. Hearts must be so cemented together, love must become so dominant that the wealthy will most willingly take steps to establish economic adjustments permanently. They themselves must realize that it is neither just nor lawful that they should possess great wealth while there is abject poverty in the community. In this way, they will willingly give of their wealth, while retaining as much as will enable them to live comfortably.

1. Read through the statement and study it in your group in the usual way. There are many issues on people's minds that relate to wealth and poverty—employment, wages, housing, to name a few. Can you think of other topics the discussion of which would benefit from the ideas in this statement?

_____

_____

_____

_____

2. What would you answer if someone who heard you mention the above ideas asked you the following: "Are you saying that the rich will come to understand and support strict tax laws, and they will willingly pay what they really should? What makes you think this is possible?"

_____

_____

_____

3. It is suggested that you memorize one or two of these quotations from the Writings of Bahá'u'lláh:

"... ye must give forth goodly and wondrous fruits, that ye yourselves and others may profit therefrom. Thus it is incumbent on every one to engage in crafts and professions, for therein lies the secret of wealth, O men of understanding!"[22]

"If thine eyes be turned towards mercy, forsake the things that profit thee and cleave unto that which will profit mankind. And if thine eyes be turned towards justice, choose thou for thy neighbor that which thou choosest for thyself."[23]

"Blessed is he who preferreth his brother before himself."[24]

"No goodly deed was or will ever be lost, for benevolent acts are treasures preserved with God for the benefit of those who act."[25]

"... take heed not to outstrip the bounds of moderation, and be numbered among the extravagant."[26]

SECTION 9

Below are some ideas that will assist you in participating in discussions on the subject of prejudice.

Prejudice in all its forms—religious, racial, gender, ethnic, economic—destroys the edifice of humanity and is opposed to the commands of God. For thousands of years humanity has suffered from war and bloodshed spurred on by one or another of these prejudices. As long as they persist, humanity will not have rest.

God has sent forth His Prophets for the sole purpose of creating love and unity. All the heavenly Books are the written word of love. If they prove to be the cause of estrangement, they have become fruitless. Therefore, religious prejudice is especially opposed to the will and command of God.

National prejudice is entirely unjustifiable. Earth is one land, one country. The lines and boundaries that separate nations are imaginary; they were not created by God. People declare a river to be a boundary line between two countries, giving each side a name, whereas the river was created for both and is a natural artery for all. Is it not imagination and ignorance which impel people to make the bounties of life the cause of war and destruction?

Racial prejudice is nothing but superstition. The color of the skin of a person is merely the result of adaptations of his or her ancestors over time to climate and environment. Character is the true criterion of humanity. Excellence does not depend upon race and color. Faith, purity of heart, good deeds and praiseworthy speech are what is acceptable at the threshold of God.

For the longest time, women have been made subordinate to men and wronged. The distinction between male and female is a requirement of the physical world; in the world of the spirit they are equal. In the estimation of God, there is no distinction as to male and female. All humankind has been endowed by Him with intelligence and perception. All have the capacity to acquire virtues. There is no circumstance today in which a person's sex provides grounds for the exercise of discrimination.

According to the words of the Old Testament, God has said, "Let us make man in our image, after our likeness." This clearly applies to women as well. The human being has been created in the image of God; that is to say, divine virtues are reflected and revealed in the human reality. This is true of all humanity. How utterly untenable it is to claim that only those of one color, ethnicity or nationality were created in the likeness of God. How absurd to imply that only the wealthy were made in His image or to think a criterion for nearness to God is a high position in society. Humanity cannot attain illumination except through the abandonment of prejudices and the acquisition of the morals of the Kingdom.

1. Study this statement as you did the previous ones and then think of some challenges your friends and neighbors have brought up in conversation that call for the elimination of prejudice.

_____

_____

_____

_____

2.　　What would you answer if someone who heard you share the above ideas asked you: "Can we have prejudice and not know it?"

_____

_____

_____

3.　　You may find occasion to include in your discussions on these ideas one or another of the following quotations from the Writings of Bahá'u'lláh:

"The earth is but one country, and mankind its citizens."[27]

"All the saplings of the world have appeared from one Tree, and all the drops from one Ocean, and all beings owe their existence to one Being."[28]

"That one indeed is a man who, today, dedicateth himself to the service of the entire human race."[29]

"The light of a good character surpasseth the light of the sun and the radiance thereof."[30]

"Man's distinction lieth not in ornaments or wealth, but rather in virtuous behavior and true understanding."[31]

"God grant you may be graciously aided under all conditions to shatter the idols of superstition and to tear away the veils of the imaginations of men."[32]

"Of all men the most negligent is he that disputeth idly and seeketh to advance himself over his brother."[33]

SECTION 10

When conversing with friends, you will often be able to draw upon the ideas in the following statement about the equality of men and women:

The physical sun, through its light and heat, reveals the reality of all things on earth. The fruit hidden in the tree appears upon its branches in response to the power of the sun. Likewise, the Sun of Truth, shining in full splendor in the spiritual sky, brings to light realities that were not apparent in the past. That is why, in this age, the principle of the equality of men and women has been fully recognized and is now an established fact.

Bahá'u'lláh has stated in the clearest terms that in the sight of God there is no distinction between men and women. The condition of inequality that has existed throughout the ages is not the result of the superiority of men; it is simply that women have not been given the same opportunity to develop all their potentialities. In spite of the prejudice against them, however, history records the lives of numerous women who have achieved the greatest of accomplishments.

One such woman was the Persian poetess, Ṭáhirih. She was born in the early part of the 1800s in a country where women were entirely subordinated to men. She was the first woman to accept the truth of God's new Revelation. As she witnessed the dawn of a new Day, she became convinced that the time had come for the reality of the equality of men and women to be recognized. She dedicated her energies to proclaiming this truth. Her knowledge and eloquence baffled the most learned men of her time. Although all the forces of an oppressive king and an ignorant and proud clergy were against her, not for a moment did she hesitate to speak the truth. And in the end, she gave her life for the Cause she had so firmly embraced.

To believe in that which God has not intended is ignorance and superstition. Today women should be allowed every opportunity to become educated and to assume a position of equality with men in all fields of human endeavor. Until the equality of men and women becomes a reality in this world, as it is in the spiritual realm, the real progress of humankind will not be possible.

1. You should, as always, study this statement in your group and practice saying the ideas. Are there any conversations you have had recently with your friends that would have benefited from the insights it offers? What were the issues under discussion?

    _____

    _____

    _____

    _____

2. What are some of the beliefs and attitudes prevalent in today's society that will have to change if women are to assume an equal position with men in all fields of endeavor?

    _____

    _____

    _____

3. Below are a few quotations from the Writings of Bahá'u'lláh that you may wish to memorize.

    "Women and men have been and will always be equal in the sight of God."[34]

    "Know ye not why We created you all from the same dust? That no one should exalt himself over the other."[35]

"In this Day the Hand of divine grace hath removed all distinctions. The servants of God and His handmaidens are regarded on the same plane."[36]

SECTION 11

The final statement you are being asked to study is on the subject of universal education:

The promotion of education is a most urgent requirement of our time. No nation can achieve prosperity unless it makes education one of its central concerns. The primary reason for the decline of a people is lack of access to knowledge.

Education must begin at infancy. It is the duty of a father and mother to do their utmost to educate their children, to refine their characters according to spiritual and moral laws, and to ensure that they are trained in the arts and sciences. Mothers are the first educators of humankind; they nurse their children at the breast of knowledge. Every child must be educated; this is not a matter that can be neglected. If the parents are able to meet the necessary expense, they must do so. Otherwise the community must provide the means for the child's education.

Education should develop in every human being the desire to achieve excellence. We should become enamored of human perfection and pursue it with passion. We should aspire to spiritual distinction, to become known for the virtues of the human world—for sincerity, loyalty, service to humanity, love and justice. We must seek to be distinguished by our efforts to promote peace and unity and to foster learning. To guide people on such a path is the real task of education.

1.   After studying this statement in your group, try to identify some of the concerns your friends have about education. How do the above ideas address their concerns?

_____

_____

_____

_____

2.   It is suggested that you memorize one or more of the following quotations from the Writings of Bahá'u'lláh:

"It is not desirable that a man be left without knowledge or skills, for he is then but a barren tree."[37]

"Bend your minds and wills to the education of the peoples and kindreds of the earth . . ."[38]

"Arts, crafts and sciences uplift the world of being, and are conducive to its exaltation."[39]

"In truth, knowledge is a veritable treasure for man, and a source of glory, of bounty, of joy, of exaltation, of cheer and gladness unto him."[40]

SECTION 12

Peace is an issue on everyone's mind. Its establishment is most urgent and vital. Now that you have given some thought to the principles outlined in the preceding statements, you may find it beneficial to reflect on the question of universal peace.

Much depends, of course, on governments to take practical steps to eliminate war. Political agreements to settle disputes and to reduce arms are essential to the pursuit of peace, as are myriad forms of international collaboration among nations. Yet, no matter how important such measures, they will not lead to enduring peace if the principles discussed earlier are not established throughout the world. Unless people learn to investigate reality and come to realize that truth is one, will not age-old animosities, we must ask ourselves, continue to persist? We all have the same origin. God keeps watch over us all and trains us all through His Manifestations. Their teachings rest on the same foundation of love and fellowship. Only when the oneness of religion is acknowledged will religious strife cease and the light of religion illumine the path to peace. Is it not necessary for science and religion to work in harmony, we must further ask, to dispel the clouds of ignorance and demonstrate the falsehood of every form of prejudice, each a mighty barrier to peace? Can a peaceful world be built, is yet another question to ask, if the present inordinate disparity between the rich and the poor is not addressed in every corner of the globe? And, not until women are allowed to move into all spheres of human endeavor on equal footing with men will the violence that has characterized so much of history give way to peace and true prosperity. Rising generations must be universally educated according to such principles, otherwise every hope for peace will be shattered. You may wish to memorize the following words of Bahá'u'lláh so that you can share them with others concerned for humanity's future:

> **"The well-being of mankind, its peace and security, are unattainable unless and until its unity is firmly established."**[41]

REFERENCES

1. *Gleanings from the Writings of Bahá'u'lláh* (Wilmette: Bahá'í Publishing Trust, 1983, 2017 printing), CIX, par. 2, p. 243.

2. Ibid., CXXXII, par. 1, p. 325.

3. Ibid., XXXIV, par. 5, p. 89.

4. *Tablets of Bahá'u'lláh Revealed after the Kitáb-i-Aqdas* (Wilmette: Bahá'í Publishing Trust, 1988, 2005 printing), no. 11.1, p. 161.

5. Bahá'u'lláh, *The Kitáb-i-Íqán: The Book of Certitude* (Wilmette: Bahá'í Publishing Trust, 2003, 2018 printing), par. 151, p. 131.

6. *Gleanings from the Writings of Bahá'u'lláh*, XXVIII, par. 2, p. 77.

7. Ibid., XXIV, par. 1, p. 66.

8. Ibid., CXI, par. 1, p. 246.

9. Ibid., XLIII, par. 6, p. 106.

10. Ibid., CX, par. 1, p. 244.

11. *Tablets of Bahá'u'lláh Revealed after the Kitáb-i-Aqdas*, no. 15.4, p. 220.

12. *Gleanings from the Writings of Bahá'u'lláh*, XCV, par. 1, pp. 219–20.

13. *Tablets of Bahá'u'lláh Revealed after the Kitáb-i-Aqdas*, no. 9.13, p. 141.

14. Ibid., no. 5.13, p. 51.

15. *Gleanings from the Writings of Bahá'u'lláh*, CXII, par. 1, pp. 247–48.

16. Ibid., CXXXII, par. 3, p. 326.

17. Ibid., CXI, par. 1, p. 246.

18. *Tablets of Bahá'u'lláh Revealed after the Kitáb-i-Aqdas*, no. 7.20, p. 90.

19. Ibid., no. 6.25, pp. 66–67.

20. Bahá'u'lláh, cited by Shoghi Effendi, *The Advent of Divine Justice* (Wilmette: Bahá'í Publishing Trust, 2006, 2018 printing), par. 42, p. 41.

21. *Tablets of Bahá'u'lláh Revealed after the Kitáb-i-Aqdas*, no. 3.23, p. 27.

22. Bahá'u'lláh, *The Hidden Words* (Wilmette: Bahá'í Publishing Trust, 2003, 2012 printing), Persian no. 80, p. 51.

23. *Tablets of Bahá'u'lláh Revealed after the Kitáb-i-Aqdas*, no. 6.19, p. 64.

24. Ibid., no. 6.37, p. 71.

25. Bahá'u'lláh, in *Ḥuqúqu'lláh—The Right of God: A Compilation of Extracts from the Writings of Bahá'u'lláh and 'Abdu'l-Bahá and from Letters Written by and on Behalf of Shoghi Effendi and the Universal House of Justice*, compiled by the Research Department of the Universal House of Justice (Wilmette: Bahá'í Publishing Trust, 2007), no. 16, p. 16.

26. *Gleanings from the Writings of Bahá'u'lláh*, CXVIII, par. 2, p. 283.

27. Ibid., CXVII, par. 1, p. 282.

28. Bahá'u'lláh, cited by Shoghi Effendi, *The Promised Day Is Come* (Wilmette: Bahá'í Publishing Trust, 1996, 2018 printing), par. 279, p. 187.

29. *Gleanings from the Writings of Bahá'u'lláh*, CXVII, par. 1, p. 282.

30. *Tablets of Bahá'u'lláh Revealed after the Kitáb-i-Aqdas*, no. 4.11, p. 36.

31. Ibid., no. 6.3, p. 57.

32. Ibid., no. 6.3, p. 58.

33. *The Hidden Words*, Persian no. 5, pp. 23–24.

34. Bahá'u'lláh, in *Women: Extracts from the Writings of Bahá'u'lláh, 'Abdu'l-Bahá, Shoghi Effendi and the Universal House of Justice*, compiled by the Research Department of the Universal House of Justice (Wilmette: Bahá'í Publishing Trust, 1986, 1997 printing), no. 54, p. 26.

35. *The Hidden Words*, Arabic no. 68, p. 20.

36. Bahá'u'lláh, in the compilation *Women*, no. 3, p. 3.

37. Bahá'u'lláh, in *Excellence in All Things: A Compilation of Extracts from the Bahá'í Writings*, compiled by the Research Department of the Universal House of Justice (London: Bahá'í Publishing Trust, 1981, 1989 printing), no. 5, p. 2.

38. *Gleanings from the Writings of Bahá'u'lláh*, CLVI, par. 1, p. 378.

39. Bahá'u'lláh, *Epistle to the Son of the Wolf* (Wilmette: Bahá'í Publishing Trust, 1988, 2016 printing), p. 26.

40. *Tablets of Bahá'u'lláh Revealed after the Kitáb-i-Aqdas*, no. 5.13, p. 52.

41. *Gleanings from the Writings of Bahá'u'lláh*, CXXXI, par. 2, p. 324.

Deepening Themes

Purpose

To develop the habit of visiting friends and neighbors
to converse on themes of spiritual significance

SECTION 1

This third unit, like the preceding one, is concerned with the capabilities that enable us to enter into meaningful and uplifting conversation. Our focus in the second unit was on the numerous occasions that present themselves to elevate the level of conversation by referring to spiritual principles. Here the focus shifts to the visits we make to the homes of friends and neighbors to explore together themes central to the life of the community.

In villages and neighborhoods throughout the world, groups of friends are intensely engaged in a set of interrelated activities that include regular devotional gatherings, classes for the spiritual education of children, meetings of junior youth, study circles, and youth camps and various kinds of campaigns. As this pattern of activity takes root in a locality and as increasing numbers dedicate themselves to acts of service, the nucleus of friends grows in size and strength. A systematic program of visits to more and more homes in the village or neighborhood is a vital component of the process of community building now gathering momentum. A diversity of themes are addressed during such visits. The teacher of a Bahá'í children's class, for example, must frequently call on the parents of the youngsters to discuss themes relevant to education. Similar visits need to be made to the homes of junior youth and youth by those serving as animators and tutors to discuss subjects bearing on the challenges and opportunities associated with these promising years in the life of a human being. Conversations held with the members of a household on themes that deepen their knowledge of the Faith prove equally essential. All in all, the effect of such visits on the culture of fellowship emerging in the community cannot be overestimated.

SECTION 2

For the purpose of this unit, we will look at an imaginary neighborhood in which the process described above is advancing, and we will use it as the context for examining the kinds of conversation that may unfold during a visit to a home.

Alejandra is a young woman in the third year of university. She and one of her brothers, also a student, live with their parents in the neighborhood we are imagining, in the house where they were born and grew up. The four of them and a young couple who recently moved to the neighborhood meet every week to pray and consult on the progress of activities being established around them within a population of some 8,000. Three others are participating from time to time in these weekly meetings and beginning to think systematically not only of their own acts of service but also of the entire community-building process: a teacher of a children's class that started six months ago and two seventeen-year-old youth who are guiding the efforts of a junior youth group with assistance from an older brother of Alejandra, who was the animator of their own group when they were younger and who visits his parents regularly.

The first set of conversations we will examine is between Alejandra and the Sanchezes, a family well-known and respected in the neighborhood. The husband and wife are in their sixties and, having raised their sons and daughters, live by themselves a few blocks away from Alejandra's home. Mr. and Mrs. Sanchez are literate but have not received a great deal of formal education. The widespread respect they enjoy is due to the wisdom they have acquired through experience in a life of generosity and pure deeds. They have been aware of the Bahá'í teachings for some time, but only recently did they decide to investigate them in earnest. A week ago, they communicated to Alejandra's parents their desire to join the community. A gathering to welcome them has already been planned and, in addition, it has been agreed that Alejandra will visit them regularly for several weeks to share with them a series of themes that will help them deepen their knowledge of the Faith. By following the account of the visits, you will be able to explore these themes and at the same time reflect on the dynamics of conversation on such occasions.

SECTION 3

Alejandra plans to base her first conversation with Mr. and Mrs. Sanchez on the brief explanation below of the theme, the eternal Covenant of God.

The Creator of all things is God, the One, the Incomparable, the Self-Subsisting. Bahá'u'lláh teaches us that the essence of God is incomprehensible to the human mind, for the finite cannot comprehend the infinite. The representations that people make of Him are but fruits of their own imaginations. God is not a man, and He is not a mere force spread throughout the universe. The words we must necessarily use to refer to the Source of our being, such as the Heavenly Father, the Heavenly Power, the Great Spirit, express His names and attributes in the human tongue and are totally inadequate to describe Him.

In the Hidden Words, we read:

"O Son of Man! I loved thy creation, hence I created thee. Wherefore, do thou love Me, that I may name thy name and fill thy soul with the spirit of life."[1]

In this passage, Bahá'u'lláh tells us that God's love for us is the very reason for our existence. We must be ever conscious of this love, which protects us, sustains us, and fills us with the spirit of life. In moments of difficulty or ease, of sadness or joy, we must remember that His love always embraces us.

From the Bahá'í teachings, we learn that, having created us out of His love, God has entered into a Covenant with us. The word "covenant" means pact or promise between two or more people. According to the eternal Covenant, the All-Bountiful Creator never abandons us and, from time to time, makes His Will and His Purpose known to us through one of His Manifestations.

The verb "to manifest" means to reveal, to show something that was not known before. The Manifestations of God are those special Beings Who reveal to us the Word of God. They are universal Educators who teach us how to live in accordance with the Will of God and how to achieve true happiness. Among these Manifestations are Abraham, Krishna, Moses, Zoroaster, Buddha, Christ, Muḥammad and, of course, the Báb and Bahá'u'lláh, the Twin Manifestations of God for this age in human history.

Thus, in the eternal Covenant of God, His part has always been fulfilled. A fundamental question we must all ask ourselves is, "How do I fulfill my part of the Covenant?" The answer we find in all religious scriptures is: by recognizing the Manifestation of God and obeying His teachings. This response points to the very purpose of our lives, which is to know and to worship God. In the Short Obligatory Prayer, we declare:

"I bear witness, O my God, that Thou hast created me to know Thee and to worship Thee. I testify, at this moment, to my powerlessness and to Thy might, to my poverty and to Thy wealth.

"There is none other God but Thee, the Help in Peril, the Self-Subsisting."[2]

Since it is impossible for us to know God except through His Manifestations, the only way we can achieve the purpose of our lives is by recognizing Them and following Their teachings. Today, our hearts overflow with gratitude for the bounty of living in a time when the promise made in all the Holy Books, that peace and justice would be established on earth, is being fulfilled. Bahá'u'lláh proclaims:

"This is the Day in which God's most excellent favors have been poured out upon men, the Day in which His most mighty grace hath been infused into all created things. It is incumbent upon all the peoples of the world to reconcile their differences, and, with perfect unity and peace, abide beneath the shadow of the Tree of His care and loving-kindness."[3]

Before we continue with our story, you should read the above explanation and reflect on it paragraph by paragraph with the other participants of your group. You can ask questions of one another and answer them together, until each of you is able to express the ideas naturally and with ease. Learning the quotations well is especially important, for sharing passages from the Writings in discussions of this kind is indispensable. The following exercises will help you think about the ideas presented in this section and on the meaning of the passages quoted:

1. How would you explain to someone that God is an unknowable essence? The first paragraph in the above should be of help to you in this respect.

     _____

     _____

     _____

     _____

2. Why did God create us? _____

     _____

3. What does the word "covenant" mean? _____

     _____

4. What has God promised in His eternal Covenant with humanity? _____

     _____

5. What is the purpose of our lives? _____

     _____

6. If we can never know the essence of God, what does it mean that the purpose of our lives is to know God? _____

_____

7. What does the word "manifest" mean? _____

_____

8. Name some of the Manifestations of God: _____

_____

_____

_____

9. What is required of us if we are to fulfill our part in the Covenant? _____

_____

10. Complete the following sentences:

   a. In this Day, God's _____ have been poured out upon humanity.

   b. In this Day, God's _____ has been infused into all created things.

   c. In this Day, we should _____ our differences, and, with perfect unity and peace, _____

   _____ .

11. What does Bahá'u'lláh ask the peoples of the world to do? _____

_____

_____

SECTION 4

The content of the theme Alejandra plans to share with Mr. and Mrs. Sanchez is not the only thing that has been on her mind. She hopes to build a strong bond of friendship with the couple. From firsthand experience, she knows the malevolent effects of both prejudice and a patronizing attitude. These she will naturally avoid; her higher studies have not lessened her humility. She has nothing in her heart but genuine love and respect for the Sanchezes. As she considers how she is going to explain the first theme, she reminds herself that this is the beginning of an ongoing conversation that will unfold over many weeks. She recognizes that, although it is important to present the sequence of ideas with clarity, she should stop at certain points to listen to the couple's response. "I should try not to be nervous," she tells herself, "because that is when I keep talking and talking, and there will be no chance for a conversation to take shape." Alejandra continues to think about her visit for some time along these lines. If you were in her place, which of the following would you regard as appropriate thoughts to enter your mind?

_____ It's my job to instruct the Sanchezes in the Faith and make sure they learn everything I teach them.

_____ What a privilege it is to be able to spend some time with this wonderful couple and share with them passages from the Writings.

_____ I know this visit is important. Still, I hope it doesn't take long because I have other things to do.

_____ The quotations will be too difficult for them. I should just mention a couple of simple ideas. What is important is to show them love.

_____ At their age, the Sanchezes cannot learn much.

_____ I am looking forward to the visit and to hearing their insights as we discuss the theme and reflect on the quotations.

_____ They can read. I'll just introduce the subject and leave them the quotations to study for themselves.

_____ When presenting ideas, I will have to pause often so that we can study the quotations together and consult about them.

_____ I hope I can present the whole theme without interruption and ask them if they have any questions at the end.

Can you think of other sentiments that you would or would not want to have in preparing for such a visit?

SECTION 5

Alejandra's first visit to the Sanchez home goes well. The couple notes her nervousness and makes her feel at ease with their warmth and kindness. They listen carefully and participate fully in the discussion, paying particular attention to the quotations. The only moment of difficulty is at the end when Mrs. Sanchez surprises Alejandra with a question: "Am I forgetting Christ by joining the Bahá'í community?" Alejandra knows the answer, but it takes her time to formulate it. Mr. Sanchez smiles and comes to her aid: "I think my love for Christ has actually grown since we have learned about the Bahá'í teachings." "And that is the way with so many throughout the world," adds Alejandra, who has gathered her thoughts together. "Their love for Moses, Christ, Krishna, Buddha, Zoroaster, and Muḥammad is strengthened because of what Bahá'u'lláh teaches about the unity of God, the unity of religion, and the unity of humankind."

It would be useful for you to take a moment in your group to discuss some of the qualities and attitudes that must have been present during Alejandra's visit to make it so fruitful. Chief among those you need to consider is humility. The foundation of all humility is humility before God. From it springs humility before His creatures. At no time is humility more important than when one speaks of God and His Manifestations. You should reflect on the following words of Bahá'u'lláh and make every effort to memorize them:

"They who are the beloved of God, in whatever place they gather and whomsoever they may meet, must evince, in their attitude towards God, and in the manner of their celebration of His praise and glory, such humility and submissiveness that every atom of the dust beneath their feet may attest the depth of their devotion. The conversation carried by these holy souls should be informed with such power that these same atoms of dust will be thrilled by its influence. They should conduct themselves in such manner that the earth upon which they tread may never be allowed to address to them such words as these: 'I am to be preferred above you. For witness, how patient I am in bearing the burden which the husbandman layeth upon me. I am the instrument that continually imparteth unto all beings the blessings with which He Who is the Source of all grace hath entrusted me. Notwithstanding the honor conferred upon me, and the unnumbered evidences of my wealth—a wealth that supplieth the needs of all creation—behold the measure of my humility, witness with what absolute submissiveness I allow myself to be trodden beneath the feet of men. . . .'"[4]

As mentioned above, humility before our fellow human beings springs from humility before God. It is with this same humility that we assume a prayerful attitude while visiting the home of a friend or neighbor to deepen our understanding of certain themes together. During the conversation, we turn our thoughts frequently towards God, asking Him to illumine our minds and hearts and those of everyone present. There are many phrases and sentences from prayers that we can memorize with this purpose in mind. These are only a few:

"Illumine our hearts, grant us discerning eyes and attentive ears."[5]

"O Lord! Grant Thine infinite bestowals, and let the light of Thy guidance shine."[6]

"Unlock the gates of true understanding and let the light of faith shine resplendent."[7]

"O Lord! Illumine our eyes so that we may behold Thy light."[8]

"Wholly unto Thee do I turn, fervently imploring Thee with all my heart, my mind and my tongue, to shield me from all that runs counter to Thy will in this, the cycle of Thy divine unity . . ."[9]

SECTION 6

Alejandra's heart is full of joy after her visit to the home of the Sanchezes and her conversation with them on the theme of the eternal Covenant. "The next visit," she thinks, "would be a good opportunity for them to deepen their knowledge of Bahá'u'lláh's life." The following is the presentation upon which she will draw:

Bahá'u'lláh was born on 12 November 1817 in Ṭihrán, the capital city of Persia. From childhood He showed extraordinary qualities, and His parents were convinced that He was destined for greatness. Bahá'u'lláh's father, a distinguished minister in the court of the king, had immense love for his Son. One night he dreamt that Bahá'u'lláh was swimming in a limitless ocean, His body shining and illuminating the vast sea. Around His head radiated His long jet-black hair, floating in all directions. A multitude of fish gathered around Him, each holding on to the extremity of one hair. Great as was the number of fish, not a single hair was detached from Bahá'u'lláh's head. He moved freely and unrestrained, and they all followed Him. Bahá'u'lláh's father asked a man renowned for his wisdom to explain the dream. He was told that the limitless ocean was the world of being. Alone and single-handed, Bahá'u'lláh would achieve sovereignty over it. The multitude of fish represented the turmoil which He would arouse among the peoples of the world. He would have the unfailing protection of the Almighty; this tumult would not harm Him.

By the time Bahá'u'lláh was thirteen or fourteen, He was famous in the court of the king for His wisdom and learning. He was twenty-two years old when His father died, and the government offered his position to Bahá'u'lláh. But He had no intention of spending His time in the management of worldly affairs. He left behind the court and its ministers to follow the path set for Him by God. He devoted His time to helping the oppressed, the sick and the poor, and soon He became known as a champion of the cause of justice.

At the age of twenty-seven, Bahá'u'lláh received, through a special messenger, some of the Writings of the Báb, Who was proclaiming the dawn of a new Day, the Day when a new Manifestation of God would bring to the world the peace, unity and justice long awaited by humanity. Bahá'u'lláh immediately accepted the Message of the Báb and became one of His most enthusiastic followers. But alas, those who ruled over the people of Persia, blinded by their own selfish desires, set out to persecute the followers of the Báb with great savagery. Bahá'u'lláh, despite being known for His nobility, was not spared. A little over eight years after the Báb's Declaration, and two years after the Báb Himself had been martyred, He was imprisoned in a dark dungeon called the Black Pit. The chains put around His neck were so heavy that He could not lift His head. Here Bahá'u'lláh spent four terrible months in severe hardship. Yet it was in this same dungeon that the Spirit of God filled His soul and revealed to Him that He was the Promised One of all ages. From this dark prison, the Sun of Bahá'u'lláh rose illuminating the entire creation.

After four months in the Black Pit, Bahá'u'lláh was stripped of all His possessions, and He and His family were sent into exile. In the bitter cold of winter, they traveled along the western mountains of Persia towards Baghdád, then a city in the Ottoman Empire and today the capital of 'Iráq. Words cannot describe their sufferings as they walked hundreds of kilometers on snow and ice-covered ground on their way to that fate-laden city.

The fame of Bahá'u'lláh soon spread throughout Baghdád and other cities of the region, and more and more people came to the door of this exiled Prisoner to receive His blessings. But there were a few who became jealous of His fame. Among them was Bahá'u'lláh's own half-brother Mírzá Yaḥyá, who was living under His loving care. Mírzá Yaḥyá's plotting caused disunity among the followers of the Báb and brought great sadness to Bahá'u'lláh. One night, without telling anyone, Bahá'u'lláh left His home and went to the mountains of Kurdistán. There He lived a secluded life engaged in prayer and meditation. He stayed in a small cave and subsisted on the simplest of foods. No one in that area knew His origin, and no one knew His name. But, then, gradually the people of the region began to speak of the "Nameless One", a great Saint who had knowledge bestowed upon Him by God. When the news of this Holy Personage reached Bahá'u'lláh's oldest Son, 'Abdu'l-Bahá, He immediately recognized the signs of His beloved Father. Letters were sent with a special messenger entreating Bahá'u'lláh to return to Baghdád. This He accepted, bringing to an end a period of painful separation that had lasted two years.

During Bahá'u'lláh's absence, the conditions of the Bábí community had declined rapidly. In the seven years He lived in Baghdád following His return from the mountains, Bahá'u'lláh infused the persecuted and confused followers of the Báb with a new spirit. Although He had not yet announced His own great station, the power and wisdom of His words began to win the loyalty of an increasing number of Bábís and the admiration of people of every walk of life. But the fanatical Muslim clergy could not bear to see the tremendous influence Bahá'u'lláh had on such a large number of souls. They complained and complained to the authorities until the government of Persia joined hands with some of the officials of the Ottoman Empire to remove Bahá'u'lláh farther away from His homeland, this time to the city of Constantinople.

April of 1863 was a month of great sadness for the population of Baghdád. The One Whom they had grown to love was leaving their city, heading for what to them was an unknown destination. Just prior to His departure, Bahá'u'lláh moved to a garden on the outskirts of the city, raised His tent and for twelve days received the stream of visitors who gathered to say farewell. The followers of the Báb came to this garden with heavy hearts; some would accompany Bahá'u'lláh on this next stage of His exile, though many would have to stay behind and be deprived of close association with Him. But God had not willed that this occasion would be one of sadness. The doors of His infinite bounty were opened wide, and Bahá'u'lláh proclaimed to those around Him that He was the One foretold by the Báb—He Whom God would make manifest. Sadness gave way to boundless joy; hearts were uplifted and souls were enkindled with the fire of His love. This twelve-day period in April is celebrated everywhere as the Festival of Riḍván, the anniversary of the declaration by Bahá'u'lláh of His world-embracing Mission.

Constantinople was the seat of the Ottoman Empire. Here again, over just four months, Bahá'u'lláh's great wisdom and personal charm began to attract an increasing number of people. "He must not stay in Constantinople any longer," murmured the fanatical Muslim clergy, who convinced the authorities to exile Him to the town of Adrianople. In Adrianople, where He remained for four and a half years, Bahá'u'lláh wrote Tablets to the kings and the rulers of the world calling on them to abandon the ways of oppression and dedicate themselves to the welfare of their people. Then His enemies conceived a most cruel punishment. He and His family would be exiled to 'Akká, which at the time was the worst penal colony in the entire empire. "Surely He will perish in the harsh conditions of that prison-city," thought the feeble-minded men who imagined they could stop the plan God Himself had set in motion.

The hardships Bahá'u'lláh suffered in 'Akká are too many to recount. He lacked every means of comfort and was surrounded by enemies day and night. But the conditions of imprisonment gradually changed. The inhabitants of 'Akká and its government became convinced of the innocence of the small band of Bahá'ís who had been exiled to their city. Once again, people were attracted by the wisdom and love of this extraordinary Personage, even though the majority did not understand His great station. After some nine years, the doors of the prison-city were opened to Bahá'u'lláh and His followers. His beloved Son 'Abdu'l-Bahá was able to secure a dignified place for His Father to live outside the city walls, and eventually it became possible for 'Abdu'l-Bahá to rent a home in the countryside where Bahá'u'lláh was able to spend the remaining thirteen years of His life in relative peace and tranquility. We now know this house as the Mansion of Bahjí, and there He passed away in May of 1892 at the height of His majesty and glory.

Bahá'u'lláh raised the banner of universal peace and fellowship and revealed the Word of God. Although His enemies combined their forces against Him, He was victorious over them as God had promised Him when under chains in the dark dungeon in Ṭihrán. During His own lifetime, His Message revived the hearts of thousands of people. And today, His teachings continue to spread throughout the world. Nothing can prevent Him from achieving His ultimate goal, which is to unify humankind in one universal Cause, in one common Faith.

The above account of the life of Bahá'u'lláh is relatively long. Before moving on to the exercises below, you should read the account paragraph by paragraph in your group and ask one another questions until you learn the content well and can present it with ease. The following map will assist you in calling to mind the path of Bahá'u'lláh's exiles and in remembering the events that occurred along the way.

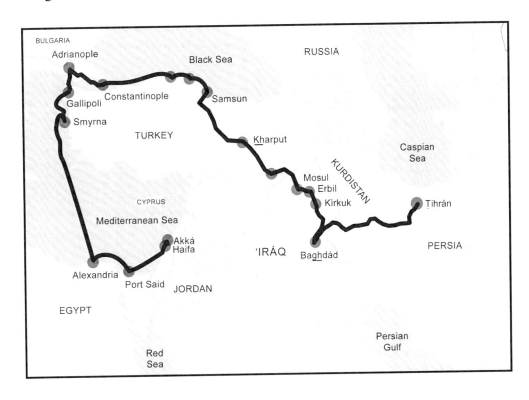

1. You may find it helpful to write down in the space provided, on the basis of the above account, the sequence of the major events associated with Bahá'u'lláh's life.

_____

_____

_____

_____

_____

_____

_____

_____

_____

_____

_____

_____

_____

_____

_____

_____

_____

_____

_____

_____

_____

_____

_____

2.   In a discussion around the theme of Bahá'u'lláh's life, there are a number of concepts that need to be underscored, apart from the sequence of events. Of particular importance is reflection on the suffering He endured out of His love for humanity, as well as on the extraordinary victories achieved by His Faith in the face of opposition. Let these words be engraved on our minds and hearts:

"The Ancient Beauty hath consented to be bound with chains that mankind may be released from its bondage, and hath accepted to be made a prisoner within this most mighty Stronghold that the whole world may attain unto true liberty. He hath drained to its dregs the cup of sorrow, that all the peoples of the earth may attain unto abiding joy, and be filled with gladness. This is of the mercy of your Lord, the Compassionate, the Most Merciful. We have accepted to be abased, O believers in the Unity of God, that ye may be exalted, and have suffered manifold afflictions, that ye might prosper and flourish. He Who hath come to build anew the whole world, behold, how they that have joined partners with God have forced Him to dwell within the most desolate of cities!"[10]

3.   When we speak about Bahá'u'lláh's suffering, we should be careful not to present Him as a helpless victim of His enemies. He willingly accepted to be bound in chains in order to free humanity. The story of His life, although filled with accounts of great suffering, is in its essence one of triumph. With the help of the tutor of your group, can you prepare a short talk on the sufferings and victories of Bahá'u'lláh based on your current knowledge of His life? The questions below may be of assistance to you.

a.   Why did Bahá'u'lláh consent to be bound with chains? _____

_____

b. Why did Bahá'u'lláh accept to be made a prisoner? _____

_____

c. Why did Bahá'u'lláh drink from the cup of sorrow? _____

_____

d. Why did Bahá'u'lláh accept to be abased? _____

_____

e. Why did Bahá'u'lláh suffer so many afflictions? _____

_____

f. Did Bahá'u'lláh accept to suffer because He was powerless to do otherwise?

_____

g. If Bahá'u'lláh was not powerless before His enemies, then why did He accept
to suffer? _____

_____

SECTION 7

Alejandra's second visit to the Sanchez home is as joyous as the first. Mr. and
Mrs. Sanchez are already somewhat familiar with the story of Bahá'u'lláh's life, but they are
happy to learn more from Alejandra's presentation and are clearly touched by the account of
His sufferings. "It seems," ponders Mrs. Sanchez at one point, "that the Manifestations of God
always suffer at the hands of those who thirst after leadership and worldly power." Alejandra
decides it is appropriate to share with them the quotation she has memorized—which you,
too, know from your study of the last section—in which Bahá'u'lláh speaks of the suffering
He endured for the sake of humanity, that we may be freed from oppression and attain lasting
happiness. All three friends feel galvanized by the discussion that day.

In contemplating her next visit, Alejandra quickly concludes that the station of
'Abdu'l-Bahá would be a natural theme for discussion. These are the points she will make
sure to cover:

> The eldest Son of Bahá'u'lláh, 'Abdu'l-Bahá is a most unique figure in human history,
> and we can find no personage like Him in any previous religion. He recognized the
> divine station of His Father while still a child and shared in His exiles and sufferings.
> It was under 'Abdu'l-Bahá's care and protection that Bahá'u'lláh left the Bahá'í
> community after His passing. We can never fully appreciate what an immense
> bounty Bahá'u'lláh bestowed upon humanity by giving us not only His most sublime
> Revelation but also His Son, through Whose knowledge and wisdom, He said, the
> world would be guided and illumined.

> When we study the life and utterances of 'Abdu'l-Bahá, we gain insight into the
> unique station that He occupies in this Dispensation. Three aspects of this station
> are important for us to keep in mind.

First, 'Abdu'l-Bahá is the Center of Bahá'u'lláh's Covenant. Bahá'u'lláh made a covenant with His followers calling upon them to direct their hearts towards that center and be entirely loyal to it. In His Will and Testament, 'Abdu'l-Bahá named Shoghi Effendi, the Guardian of the Faith, to be the center to which all should turn after His passing. Today, this center is the Universal House of Justice, which has been established in accordance with the explicit command of Bahá'u'lláh and the clear instructions given by 'Abdu'l-Bahá and the Guardian. The power of the Covenant holds the Bahá'í community together and protects it from division and disintegration.

Second, 'Abdu'l-Bahá is the unerring Interpreter of Bahá'u'lláh's words. So vast is the Revelation of Bahá'u'lláh, so profound the meanings enshrined in His utterances, that He deemed it necessary to leave behind an interpreter, One Whom He would Himself inspire. Thus, for generations to come, humanity will be able to understand Bahá'u'lláh's teachings by studying the interpretations of 'Abdu'l-Bahá in His numerous Tablets and in the authenticated transcripts of His talks. The Guardian was the Interpreter of Bahá'u'lláh's teachings after 'Abdu'l-Bahá; with him the task of interpretation was complete, and no one has the authority to interpret Bahá'u'lláh's words for the remainder of His Dispensation.

In the past, every religion has been afflicted with divisions over the different interpretations of passages from its Sacred Scriptures. But in this Dispensation, when there is uncertainty about the meaning of a statement of Bahá'u'lláh, everyone turns to the interpretations of 'Abdu'l-Bahá and the Guardian. If uncertainty remains, one can turn to the Universal House of Justice for clarification. No room is left, then, for conflict over the meaning of the teachings, and the unity of the Faith is protected.

Third, 'Abdu'l-Bahá is the perfect Exemplar of His Father's teachings. Although we can never hope to reach such a degree of perfection, we should always have Him before our eyes and strive to follow His example. When we read in the Writings about love, we can turn to 'Abdu'l-Bahá and we will see the very essence of love and kindness. When we read about purity, justice, rectitude, joy and generosity, we can turn to Him and think of His life, and we will see how He manifested these qualities to the utmost perfection.

The mark of 'Abdu'l-Bahá's life was, of course, His servitude. The name 'Abdu'l-Bahá means "the servant of Bahá", and this was the title He preferred over all the others that were attributed to Him. The following words of 'Abdu'l-Bahá are the expression of His ardent desire to serve:

"My name is 'Abdu'l-Bahá. My qualification is 'Abdu'l-Baha. My reality is 'Abdu'l-Bahá. My praise is 'Abdu'l-Bahá. Thraldom to the Blessed Perfection is my glorious and refulgent diadem, and servitude to all the human race my perpetual religion . . . No name, no title, no mention, no commendation have I, nor will ever have, except 'Abdu'l-Bahá. This is my longing. This is my greatest yearning. This is my eternal life. This is my everlasting glory."[11]

Clearly what Alejandra plans to share with the Sanchezes in her next visit is no more than an introduction to a most unique figure; their appreciation of the station occupied by 'Abdu'l-Bahá in this Dispensation will continue to grow in the years to come. In your own life, as you walk the path of service, you will have many opportunities to call His example to mind and to reflect on His words. Already, in the previous unit, you familiarized yourself with some of His utterances, and you were encouraged to learn to express in the manner He did ideas set forth in His Tablets and public talks. For now, to consolidate your present understanding of His station, you should consult with the other members of your group on the main points mentioned above and practice saying them well. Reflection on the passage quoted will inspire you in your efforts to advance on the path of service.

SECTION 8

A question that has been on Alejandra's mind since she began her visits with Mr. and Mrs. Sanchez is what themes of discussion will help them most to become confirmed and active protagonists of the community-building process in the neighborhood. On the one hand, there are themes like prayer, the immortality of the soul, and steadfastness in the love of God that she hopes to discuss with them, for the foundations of their spiritual life must be continually reinforced. On the other, it will be important for them to gain a vision of the kind of community that is gradually being developed and know that they can make valuable contributions to its realization. During her conversation with Mr. and Mrs. Sanchez about the station of 'Abdu'l-Bahá, Alejandra gradually comes to realize what the theme of her next visit should be. "They have a great deal of clarity about the purpose of the Faith to unite people," she thinks. "So, the theme we should probably explore now is how to build and maintain a unified community."

Alejandra begins her fourth visit by describing the activities that are currently being undertaken by a relatively small group of friends in the neighborhood. "As our numbers increase," she explains, "the most challenging responsibility we all must shoulder will be to become more and more united in our words, in our thoughts, and in our actions. If you agree, then, today we can explore the theme of unity together."

"I can see how important unity is to the development of our community," responds Mrs. Sanchez.

"And after all it was Bahá'u'lláh's message of unity that first attracted our hearts to His teachings," says Mr. Sanchez.

"I have chosen a number of ideas and have found a quotation for each," says Alejandra. "If you don't mind, we can go through them one by one and discuss them."

Below is Alejandra's list of ideas:

- For our community to be truly united, every one of us must avoid strife and contention. Bahá'u'lláh states:

  "Nothing whatever can, in this Day, inflict a greater harm upon this Cause than dissension and strife, contention, estrangement and apathy, among the loved ones of God. Flee them, through the power of God and His sovereign aid, and strive ye to knit together the hearts of men, in His Name, the Unifier, the All-Knowing, the All-Wise."[12]

- We should have love for everyone in the community, a love that is a reflection of our love for God. 'Abdu'l-Bahá says:

"Be in perfect unity. Never become angry with one another. . . . Love the creatures for the sake of God and not for themselves. You will never become angry or impatient if you love them for the sake of God. Humanity is not perfect. There are imperfections in every human being, and you will always become unhappy if you look toward the people themselves. But if you look toward God, you will love them and be kind to them, for the world of God is the world of perfection and complete mercy."[13]

• If, with all the love we feel for one another, tensions arise among us, we should immediately remember this counsel of 'Abdu'l-Bahá:

"I charge you all that each one of you concentrate all the thoughts of your heart on love and unity. When a thought of war comes, oppose it by a stronger thought of peace. A thought of hatred must be destroyed by a more powerful thought of love. Thoughts of war bring destruction to all harmony, well-being, restfulness and content.

"Thoughts of love are constructive of brotherhood, peace, friendship, and happiness."[14]

• And if, having made every effort to control them, we see our passions overtaking us and find ourselves in conflict with others, we should remind ourselves of these words of Bahá'u'lláh:

"If any differences arise amongst you, behold Me standing before your face, and overlook the faults of one another for My name's sake and as a token of your love for My manifest and resplendent Cause."[15]

• The spiritual discipline of overlooking the faults of others, focusing on their praiseworthy qualities and abstaining totally from backbiting is a most effective measure against disunity. Overcoming the inclination to backbite is easier when we love one another. We should remember that we tend not to see the faults of those we love and have no difficulty looking upon them with a sin-covering eye. 'Abdu'l-Bahá says:

"The imperfect eye beholds imperfections. The eye that covers faults looks toward the Creator of souls. He created them, trains and provides for them, endows them with capacity and life, sight and hearing; therefore, they are the signs of His grandeur. You must love and be kind to everybody, care for the poor, protect the weak, heal the sick, teach and educate the ignorant."[16]

Bahá'u'lláh exhorts us:

"O Companion of My Throne! Hear no evil, and see no evil, abase not thyself, neither sigh and weep. Speak no evil, that thou mayest not hear it spoken unto thee, and magnify not the faults of others that thine own faults may not appear great; and wish not the abasement of anyone, that thine own abasement be not exposed. Live then the days of thy life, that are less than a fleeting moment, with thy mind stainless, thy heart unsullied, thy thoughts pure, and thy nature sanctified, so that, free and content, thou mayest put away this mortal frame, and repair unto the mystic paradise and abide in the eternal kingdom forevermore."[17]

And He tells us:

"O Emigrants! The tongue I have designed for the mention of Me, defile it not with detraction. If the fire of self overcome you, remember your own faults and not the faults of My creatures, inasmuch as every one of you knoweth his own self better than he knoweth others."[18]

- Unity is not merely the absence of strife and dissension, and love is not to be expressed in words alone. We can only claim that true unity exists among us if our love for one another is translated into service to the community and if our activities are governed by a spirit of cooperation and mutual aid. 'Abdu'l-Bahá calls upon us:

"Rest not, even for an instant, and seek not comfort, even for a moment; rather labor with heart and soul that thou mayest render devoted service to but one amongst the friends and bring happiness and joy to but one luminous heart. This is true bounty, and by it the brow of 'Abdu'l-Bahá is illumined. Be thou my partner and associate therein."[19]

And He states:

"The supreme need of humanity is cooperation and reciprocity. The stronger the ties of fellowship and solidarity amongst men, the greater will be the power of constructiveness and accomplishment in all the planes of human activity."[20]

- A most important key to successful community action is frank and loving consultation on all matters. Through consultation, the various ways we each look at an issue merge together, and we discover what direction we should follow in our collective actions. Through consultation, we achieve unity of thought, and with our thoughts and views united, we create effective plans for the progress of our communities. 'Abdu'l-Bahá says of those who consult:

"The prime requisites for them that take counsel together are purity of motive, radiance of spirit, detachment from all else save God, attraction to His Divine Fragrances, humility and lowliness amongst His loved ones, patience and long-suffering in difficulties and servitude to His exalted Threshold. Should they be graciously aided to acquire these attributes, victory from the unseen Kingdom of Bahá shall be vouchsafed to them."[21]

- Unity of thought is unfulfilled if it is not translated into unity of action. Acting in unity does not mean that we all do the same thing. On the contrary, in unified action the diverse talents of the members of a community are used to the fullest. Our powers multiply, and even when our numbers are still small, we are able to achieve what most large and powerful organizations in the world are incapable of accomplishing. 'Abdu'l-Bahá says:

"Whensoever holy souls, drawing on the powers of heaven, shall arise with such qualities of the spirit, and march in unison, rank on rank, every one of those souls will be even as one thousand, and the surging waves of that mighty ocean will be even as the battalions of the Concourse on high."[22]

After you have read the above carefully and discussed the content point by point with the participants in your group, you will want to help one another practice presenting the theme as you have done with the previous three. You will find the exercises below of some assistance to your efforts.

1. Complete the following sentences:

    a. Nothing whatever can, in this Day, inflict a greater harm upon this Cause than _____ and strife, contention, estrangement and apathy, among the loved ones of God.

    b. Nothing whatever can, in this Day, inflict a greater harm upon this Cause than dissension and _____ , contention, estrangement and apathy, among the loved ones of God.

    c. _____ whatever can, in this Day, inflict a greater harm upon this Cause than dissension and strife, contention, estrangement and apathy, among the loved ones of God.

    d. Nothing whatever can, in this Day, inflict a greater harm upon this Cause than dissension and strife, contention, estrangement and _____ , among the loved ones of God.

    e. Nothing whatever can, in this Day, inflict a greater harm upon this Cause than dissension and strife, _____ , estrangement and apathy, among the loved ones of God.

    f. Nothing whatever can, in this Day, inflict a greater harm upon this Cause than dissension and strife, contention, _____ and apathy, among the loved ones of God.

    g. Nothing whatever can, in this Day, inflict a greater harm upon this _____ than dissension and strife, contention, estrangement and apathy, among the loved ones of God.

2. In the second quotation, 'Abdu'l-Bahá tells us:

    a. We must live in perfect _____ .

    b. We must never become _____ with _____ .

    c. We must love all people for the _____ and not for themselves.

    d. We will never become _____ or _____ if we love people for the _____ .

e. Humanity is not _____ .

f. We will always become _____ if we look toward _____

_____ .

g. If we look toward _____ , we will _____ people and be

_____ to them.

3. In the third quotation, 'Abdu'l-Bahá tells us:

a. We must each concentrate all the thoughts of our heart on _____

and _____ .

b. When a thought of war comes, we should oppose it by _____

_____ .

c. A thought of hatred can be destroyed by _____

_____ .

d. Thoughts of war bring destruction to all _____ , _____ ,

_____ and _____ .

e. Thoughts of love are constructive of _____ , _____ ,

_____ , and _____ .

4. What should you do when you see differences arising between yourself and others
in the community? _____

_____

_____

_____

5. Describe the spiritual discipline that helps you contribute towards unity in your
community: _____

_____

_____

_____

6. Which of the following contribute to unity?

____ Looking at the shortcomings of others

____ Overlooking the faults of others

____ Commenting on the shortcomings of another person to a friend

____ Exaggerating or changing a story to make another person look bad

____ Thinking of the faults of others

7. Why do we criticize some people when they make a mistake, but not others when they do the exact same thing? _____

_____

_____

_____

8. Is it possible to have unity in a situation where people are backbiting about one another? Why not? _____

_____

_____

_____

_____

9. To tell a lie about someone is obviously wrong. But is it all right to make critical remarks about someone to others for something he or she has actually done? ____

_____

10. What is the difference between gossiping, backbiting, and criticizing others? ____

_____

_____

_____

_____

11. What effects do gossip, backbiting, and constant criticism have on a community?

_____

_____

_____

_____

12. How can we eliminate these habits from our lives? _____

_____

_____

_____

13. What would happen if we only spoke about people as though they were present?

_____

_____

_____

14.   If we backbite in front of children, what effect will it have on them? _____

_____

_____

_____

15.   Where does the tendency to gossip and engage in backbiting come from? _____

_____

_____

16.   Bahá'u'lláh exhorts us: "If the fire of self overcome you, _____

_____ and not _____ ,

inasmuch as every one of you knoweth _____ better than he

_____ ."

17.   Love is not merely expressed in words. What else is needed? _____

_____

18.   In relation to unity and love, 'Abdu'l-Bahá calls upon us: "_____ not, even

for an instant, and _____ not _____ , even for a moment; rather

_____ with _____ that thou mayest render

_____ to but one amongst the friends and _____

_____ to but one luminous heart."

19.   And He further states: "The supreme need of humanity is _____

and _____ . The stronger the ties of _____ and

_____ amongst men, the greater will be the power of _____

and _____ in all the planes of human activity."

20.   What is the most important key to successful community action? _____

_____

21.   'Abdu'l-Bahá says of those who consult: "The prime requisites for them that take

counsel together are _____ , _____

_____ , _____ ,

_____ , _____

_____ amongst His loved ones, _____

_____ in difficulties and _____ to His exalted

Threshold. Should they be graciously aided to acquire these attributes, _____

from the unseen Kingdom of Bahá shall be _____ ."

22.   Regarding the power of working in unity, 'Abdu'l-Bahá tells us: "Whensoever holy souls, drawing on the _____ , shall arise with such _____ , and march _____ , rank on rank, _____ of those souls will be even as _____ , and the surging waves of that mighty ocean will be even as the _____ of the _____ ."

SECTION 9

During her fourth visit with Mr. and Mrs. Sanchez, Alejandra has the pleasure of meeting Beatrice, a granddaughter who has come to live with them while attending a nearby high school. Beatrice is very curious about the theme of unity and enthusiastically participates in the discussion. As the conversation draws to a close, Mrs. Sanchez brings out some coffee and cake for everyone. This gives Alejandra an opportunity to get to know Beatrice a little better, and she arranges to meet her the next day to talk about the community-building efforts in the neighborhood. "She may be interested in studying the main sequence of courses," Alejandra thinks to herself. "I could help her go through the first few books at a steady pace. She may then want to start a children's class or assist me with the junior youth group forming in the neighborhood. In that case, she could gradually take on more responsibility for the group as she advances all the way up to Book 5, which will prepare her to serve as an animator." Alejandra has attended several gatherings for youth which, focused on certain topics of discussion, have led to the participation of many in the institute process. She decides she will follow the same sequence of ideas in her conversation with Beatrice the next day. This is how the conversation opens:

All of us want to see the world become a better place. We look forward to a future when universal peace has been established and the human family lives in harmony. Such a future is not a dream and can be built as more and more of us exert effort to contribute to the betterment of the world. Deep in our hearts each of us has the desire to serve our communities. What we need is to develop our capacity to undertake selfless acts of service for the common good.

We can think about our service to humanity by imagining a path of service on which we walk together. This path is open to all. We each make the choice to enter it, and we advance on it at our own pace. We do not walk this path alone; we serve alongside our friends, learning together and accompanying one another. Every step we take generates joy and assurance, and every effort we make brings divine confirmations.

Beatrice likes what she is hearing, and a lively conversation ensues after this short presentation. Before going any further, let us pause here and reflect on the nature of the interaction between the two new friends. Alejandra has decided to engage in a conversation of substance in order to invite Beatrice to participate in the institute process. Why would it not have been sufficient for her to simply tell Beatrice that a series of courses are being offered by the institute and invite her to join them?

_____

_____

_____

_____

_____

_____

_____

_____

SECTION 10

The conversation between Alejandra and Beatrice continues for some two hours. Below are several additional ideas Alejandra shares with her new friend. We understand, of course, that she does not make a long uninterrupted presentation. Much of the two hours is spent deliberating together on the ideas outlined in these paragraphs:

We are young, we have energy, and we have great enthusiasm. People assume we are carefree. But it is the opposite; we are concerned with the plight of humanity and would like to see real change brought to society. And we must also think about our own lives—education, work, friends, family. Each year as we grow older, we find ourselves shouldering more responsibilities; our parents expect much from us. Sometimes, when I think of all my responsibilities, I feel overwhelmed. Then I remember a quote from the Bahá'í writings I have memorized: "Man's life has its springtime and is endowed with marvelous glory. The period of youth is characterized by strength and vigor and stands out as the choicest time in human life."

What I would like to share with you is that many young people around the world in communities like ours are realizing that their energies can be directed by a twofold purpose: to take charge of their own intellectual and spiritual growth and to contribute to the transformation of society. These two aspects of our purpose are interconnected. As we develop our own capabilities, we are better able to serve others, and in helping one another, we grow as individuals and strengthen the qualities we possess.

This is where the idea of a path of service I mentioned before comes in. Walking it is not something we just add to our lives; it brings meaning to everything we do. Service to the community helps us to understand better the purpose of our education, to clarify our thoughts about the future, to develop the qualities we need to contribute to the well-being of our families. It strengthens our friendships. It keeps us from dissipating our energies on trivial pursuits.

In thinking about our spiritual and intellectual growth, we must be aware of the many forces that influence us. Some of them, like the forces of knowledge, of justice, and of love, move us in the right direction, and we must learn to align ourselves with them. Others, like the forces of materialism and self-centeredness, do the opposite, and we should resist them. We must strive to achieve excellence and have faith that our efforts will be blessed with divine confirmation.

And in thinking about our contributions to the transformation of society—transforming a world of violence, poverty, and suffering into a world of peace, prosperity, and harmony—we must consider both material and spiritual progress. Material progress for all people will not be attained if we do not make spiritual progress as well. Only if these two go hand in hand will the betterment of the world be achieved. There is another quotation I have committed to memory: "Material civilization is like unto the lamp, while spiritual civilization is the light in that lamp. If the material and spiritual civilization become united, then we will have the light and the lamp together, and the outcome will be perfect."

As we walk the path of service, we learn to work with groups of individuals, particularly children and junior youth, helping them to acquire knowledge, skills, and spiritual qualities. We also learn to pay attention to the unity of our communities. Individuals, families, and organizations that wish to contribute to the progress of a community must collaborate. They must build a shared vision and purpose and leave behind the ways of conflict.

It is important, then, that as youth we develop the habits of harmonious interaction with others. We need to be friends: accompanying one another in the work we do, accepting each other's contributions, encouraging and supporting one another, seeing each other's strengths, seeking and giving useful advice to each other, and taking joy in the accomplishments of one another. In treading the path of service, we must act, reflect on our actions, consult and study together.

Over the past few decades, the Bahá'í community has succeeded in establishing a very special kind of institution of learning in practically every country of the world. These institutes, which is how we refer to them, offer courses that strengthen our capabilities to serve the community. By studying these courses, we gain the spiritual insights and the practical skills needed to move forward on the path of service together. As we advance through them, our capacity to carry out increasingly complex acts of service grows. All along, we are accompanied by those who are more experienced than we are and, in time, we naturally come to accompany friends with less experience. From the start, we are all protagonists of personal and social transformation, eagerly assuming responsibility for our own learning and for service to the community.

"To be a protagonist" means to have the will to act thoughtfully, to persevere in our endeavors, and to gain and apply knowledge at every step. A protagonist is not a mere passive receiver of benefits but an active contributor to progress. To be a protagonist one must learn to exercise creative and disciplined initiative. The institute courses help us enhance our capacity to be protagonists of the community-building process.

We should take a moment to reflect on the ideas in the above paragraphs. As mentioned at the beginning of the section, Alejandra would not simply present the ideas one after the other but would make sure that Beatrice has ample opportunity to think about them and contribute to the discussion. What you may wish to consider—after you have had a chance to discuss every paragraph in your group and have learned to express the ideas well yourself—is whether the conversation has developed to the point that Alejandra would feel confident in sharing a few words about some of the courses of the Ruhi Institute and in inviting Beatrice to join the study of Book 1. Can you write down in the space below what you would say if you were in her place? How would you describe Books 1 and 2 and the acts of service they call for? A brief reference to acts of service taken up in subsequent books—particularly to teaching classes for the spiritual education of children and to guiding a junior youth group as its animator—would undoubtedly help Beatrice gain a vision of what service she could render in the future. The tutor of your group can assist you in writing a few sentences on these two acts of service, similar to what Alejandra might add in inviting Beatrice to study Book 1.

_____

_____

_____

_____

_____

_____

_____

_____

_____

_____

_____

_____

SECTION 11

Two weeks pass before Alejandra makes her next visit to the Sanchez home. During that time, Beatrice was able to participate in an intensive campaign and complete the first two units of Book 1. She is now going through the third unit with a group of five friends that meets twice a week in the neighborhood. Alejandra thinks it is opportune to converse with the Sanchez family on the theme of prayer and asks Beatrice whether she would like to assist her. You have yourself studied the second unit of Book 1, so there is no need to summarize for you here the content covered by Alejandra and Beatrice during the visit. After reviewing the unit, you should be able to set out the main points you would try to address in a discussion around this theme. Below is space for you to write down your ideas.

_____

_____

_____

_____

_____

_____

_____

_____

_____

_____

_____

_____

_____

_____

_____

_____

_____

_____

_____

_____

_____

_____

_____

_____

_____

_____

_____

_____

_____

_____

_____

SECTION 12

Alejandra's visits to the Sanchez family continue for some weeks to come, and they have an opportunity to discuss several themes that flow naturally from their deliberations on the significance of prayer—the life of the soul, the development of spiritual qualities, obedience to the laws and ordinances of God and steadfastness in His love. On one occasion, they also converse a little about the institutions of the Administrative Order, particularly about Local and National Spiritual Assemblies. We need not consider the content covered during each of these subsequent visits. There are, however, two questions that often arise among participants in a series of conversations such as the one we are envisioning. The first has to do with the nature of meetings held by the community and the second with financial resources. We will take up the subject of meetings, specifically the Nineteen Day Feast, in this section and look at the question of finances in the next.

The following points, then, could form the basis for a conversation on the theme of the Nineteen Day Feast:

- In the Bahá'í community, gatherings are held for various purposes—to pray, to study, to celebrate special occasions, to consult on community affairs and service to society, to discuss plans of action. Bahá'u'lláh makes the following promise:

   "By My life and My Cause! Round about whatever dwelling the friends of God may enter, and from which their cry shall rise as they praise and glorify the Lord, shall circle the souls of true believers and all the favored angels."[23]

- Listening to the Word of God in gatherings among friends brings joy to the hearts and strengthens bonds of unity. Bahá'u'lláh exhorts us:

   "It behooveth the friends in whatever land they be, to gather together in meetings, and therein to speak wisely and with eloquence, and to read the verses of God; for it is God's Words that kindle love's fire and set it ablaze."[24]

   'Abdu'l-Bahá writes:

   "Hold gatherings and recite and chant the heavenly Teachings, that perchance that country may be illumined with the light of truth and that land may, through the confirmations of the Holy Spirit, become even as a delectable paradise, for this age is the century of the All-Glorious Lord, and the melody of the oneness of the world of humanity is reaching the ears throughout the East and the West."[25]

- Of all Bahá'í meetings, the Nineteen Day Feast deserves particular mention. The Bahá'í calendar consists of nineteen months of nineteen days each, and, in every locality, Bahá'ís gather together once a month for this meeting as enjoined by Bahá'u'lláh Himself:

   "Verily, it is enjoined upon you to offer a feast, once in every month, though only water be served; for God hath purposed to bind hearts together, albeit through both earthly and heavenly means."[26]

- The Nineteen Day Feast consists of three parts. The first is the devotional part, during which prayers are recited and passages from the Sacred Writings read. The second is the administrative part, during which consultation on the affairs of the community takes place. The third is the social part.

- We get a glimpse of the importance of the devotional part of the Nineteen Day Feast from the following words of 'Abdu'l-Bahá:

   "O ye loyal servants of the Ancient Beauty! In every cycle and dispensation, the feast hath been favored and loved, and the spreading of a table for the lovers of God hath been considered a praiseworthy act. This is especially the case today, in this dispensation beyond compare, this most generous of ages, when it is highly acclaimed, for it is truly accounted among such gatherings as are held to worship and glorify God. Here the holy verses, the heavenly odes and laudations are intoned, and the heart is quickened, and carried away from itself."[27]

- During the administrative part of the Feast, the friends gathered hear reports of the activities of Bahá'í communities near and far, consult on the affairs of the Faith in their own community and on their contributions to the well-being of society, become familiar with guidance received from the Universal House of Justice, reflect on the progress of their plans, and offer suggestions to the institutions of the Faith. Consultations at the Nineteen Day Feast are of the utmost importance, for, through this means, every individual is able to participate in the affairs of the worldwide Bahá'í community.

- As to the social part of the Feast, this is time for comradeship and hospitality. Music can be played, uplifting talks given, and presentations made by the children. In short, carefully selected expressions of culture, at once dignified and joyful, can be used to enrich this part of the Feast.

- The Nineteen Day Feast is a significant feature of the Administrative Order of the Faith. It brings together the devotional, administrative, and social aspects of community life. All these aspects should be equally emphasized, for the success of the Feast depends on the right balance among these three components. In a message written in August 1989, the Universal House of Justice states:

"The World Order of Bahá'u'lláh encompasses all units of human society; integrates the spiritual, administrative and social processes of life; and canalizes human expression in its varied forms towards the construction of a new civilization. The Nineteen Day Feast embraces all these aspects at the very base of society. Functioning in the village, the town, the city, it is an institution of which all the people of Bahá are members. It is intended to promote unity, ensure progress, and foster joy."[28]

- Such an important event as the Nineteen Day Feast cannot be put together in haste. Through prayer and reflection, each individual must spiritually prepare himself or herself for the Feast, and during the event itself, everyone should participate with heart and mind, whether reading in the devotional part or merely listening to the passages being recited; whether giving reports, receiving guidance, or making suggestions; whether acting as the host or simply partaking of his or her hospitality with joy and radiance. In the same letter on the Nineteen Day Feast, the Universal House of Justice states:

"Important aspects of the preparation of the Feast include the proper selection of readings, the assignment, in advance, of good readers, and a sense of decorum both in the presentation and the reception of the devotional program. Attention to the environment in which the Feast is to be held, whether indoors or outdoors, greatly influences the experience. Cleanliness, arrangement of the space in practical and decorative ways—all play a significant part. Punctuality is also a measure of good preparation.

"To a very large extent, the success of the Feast depends on the quality of the preparation and participation of the individual. The beloved Master offers the following advice: 'Give ye great weight to the Nineteen Day gatherings, so that on these occasions the beloved of the Lord and the handmaids of the Merciful may turn their faces toward the Kingdom, chant the communes, beseech God's help, become joyfully enamored each of the other, and grow in purity and holiness, and in the fear of God, and in resistance to passion and self. Thus will they separate themselves from this elemental world, and immerse themselves in the ardors of the spirit.'"[29]

As always, you should read through the above ideas several times and discuss them in your group so that you learn to say them with ease. The following exercises will help you gain further insight into the signficance of the Nineteen Day Feast:

1.   What does Bahá'u'lláh assure us will characterize every dwelling in which we gather together to praise and glorify the Lord? _____

    _____

2.   In the second quotation above, Bahá'u'lláh tells us that, when we come together in meetings, we should speak _____ and with _____ , and read the _____ ; for it is God's Words that _____ _____ and _____ .

3.   In the third quotation above, 'Abdu'l-Bahá advises us to hold gatherings and recite and chant the heavenly Teachings, that

    −   the country in which we live may be _____ .

    −   the land where we reside may become _____ _____ .

4.   How many months are there in the Bahá'í calendar? _____

5.   How many days are in each month? _____

6.   What special gathering takes place among Bahá'ís once a month? _____

    _____

7.   What are the three parts of the Nineteen Day Feast? _____

    _____

    _____

8.   Are the parts of the Nineteen Day Feast carried out in any order? _____

9.   What is the purpose of the devotional part of the Feast? _____

    _____

    _____

    _____

    _____

10.   What is the purpose of the administrative part of the Feast? _____

    _____

_____

_____

_____

11.   What is the purpose of the social part of the Feast?   _____

_____

_____

_____

_____

12.   Which of the following topics would it be appropriate to discuss during the administrative part of the Feast?

_____ The financial needs of community undertakings

_____ The scores of the national football team

_____ How to solve a disagreement between two members of the community

_____ The progress of Bahá'í children's classes in the community

_____ The meaning of a passage from the Writings one of the members of the community was studying earlier in the week

_____ The vibrancy of the junior youth program in the community

_____ Local job opportunities opening up for young people

_____ The support the community can provide to junior youth groups whose service projects have become complex

_____ Visits to parents of children and junior youth in the educational programs promoted by the institute

_____ The strengthening of the devotional character of the community

_____ The schedule of shows being aired on television

_____ The insights that have been gained about fostering a joyful and disciplined atmosphere in study circles

_____ The celebration of the upcoming Holy Day

_____ Initiatives of social action arising from the community-building process

13.   Discuss the following question with your group: Why is balance among the three parts of the Feast so important?

14.   Now discuss the two questions below.

a. How would you prepare for the Feast if you were hosting it?

b. How would you prepare for the Feast if you were only participating in it?

SECTION 13

The second question that often arises in conversations about the Faith is how the Bahá'í community meets its financial needs. Here are a few points that may help you respond to such queries:

- The instrument that the Bahá'í community uses to take care of its material needs is the Bahá'í Fund. It is administered by the institutions of the Faith at different levels: local, national, continental, and international. Bahá'ís believe they should themselves shoulder the expenses of endeavors to promote their Faith, and therefore the Fund receives contributions only from members of the community.

- Contributing to the Fund is a voluntary act. It is confidential in the sense that it is a matter between the individual and the institutions of the Faith; names of contributors and amounts given are not announced. No pressure is placed on the members of the community to contribute. The institutions make general appeals to the community, remind it of the importance of the Fund, and point out its requirements. Not infrequently, a community will set a contribution goal for itself. But amounts are never fixed for individuals, and money is not solicited. It is left to each individual to decide, according to his or her understanding of the principles involved, how much to contribute.

- The civilization we are trying to build will be a prosperous one, both materially and spiritually. Wealth is acceptable only if certain conditions are met. We should acquire it through honest work. We should spend it for the good of humanity. And the entire community should be uplifted; it is not acceptable for a few to be extremely rich while the majority are in want of the bare necessities of life. Bahá'u'lláh tells us:

"The best of men are they that earn a livelihood by their calling and spend upon themselves and upon their kindred for the love of God, the Lord of all worlds."[30]

". . . ye must give forth goodly and wondrous fruits, that ye yourselves and others may profit therefrom. Thus it is incumbent on every one to engage in crafts and professions, for therein lies the secret of wealth, O men of understanding!"[31]

And 'Abdu'l-Bahá explains:

"Wealth is most commendable, provided the entire population is wealthy. If, however, a few have inordinate riches while the rest are impoverished, and no fruit or benefit accrues from that wealth, then it is only a liability to its possessor."[32]

- To build a society that is free from injustice and misery, we must all be generous and giving. Even if our financial resources are meager, we should still contribute something towards the progress of humanity, for true prosperity can only be achieved through giving. Generosity is a quality of the human soul; it has nothing to do with our material circumstances. In the Hidden Words, Bahá'u'lláh says:

"To give and to be generous are attributes of Mine; well is it with him that adorneth himself with My virtues."[33]

- We should remember that the true source of whatever wealth we possess is God, the All-Bountiful. He provides us with our means of existence; He makes it possible for us to progress. And when we contribute to the Fund, we are spending for His Cause a portion of what He has given to us. For Bahá'ís, then, giving to the Fund is not merely a matter of generosity; it is also a spiritual bounty and a great individual responsibility. The Guardian advises us:

"We must be like the fountain or spring that is continually emptying itself of all that it has and is continually being refilled from an invisible source. To be continually giving out for the good of our fellows undeterred by fear of poverty and reliant on the unfailing bounty of the Source of all wealth and all good—this is the secret of right living."[34]

You will have an opportunity to consider some of the ideas here in greater depth in a later course in this sequence, which addresses the subject of material means. For now, you are encouraged, as always, to discuss the content above point by point and to carry out the following exercises so that you learn to express the ideas naturally and with ease:

1.   On the basis of the quotations, fill in the blanks in the sentences below.

    a.   Bahá'u'lláh tells us that we should earn a _____ by our calling and spend it upon _____ .

    b.   We should give forth _____ and _____ fruits, that we ourselves and others _____ .

    c.   Every one of us should _____ in _____ and _____ , for therein lies the _____ of _____ .

    d.   'Abdu'l-Bahá explains that wealth is _____ , provided the _____ is wealthy.

    e.   If _____ have inordinate _____ while the _____ are _____ , and no _____ or _____ comes from that _____ , then it is only a _____ to the _____ .

    f.   Bahá'u'lláh says, "To _____ and to be _____ are attributes of Mine; well is it with him that _____ himself with My _____ ."

    g.   And the Guardian encourages us to be like the _____ or _____ that is continually _____ of all that it has and is continually _____ .

    h.   To be continually _____ for the _____ of our fellows _____ by _____ and reliant on the _____ _____ —this is the secret of right living.

2. Write down the sequence of ideas followed in the above presentation:

_____

_____

_____

_____

_____

_____

_____

_____

_____

_____

_____

_____

_____

_____

_____

_____

_____

_____

_____

_____

SECTION 14

To gain insight into the kinds of conversation that can unfold in a village or neighborhood teeming with activity, we have followed the efforts of Alejandra, a young university student. Over a series of visits, spanning several weeks, she has discussed with Mr. and Mrs. Sanchez a number of themes that, she hopes, will help deepen their knowledge of the Faith and strengthen their commitment to the teachings they have embraced. Eventually, the arrival on the scene of Beatrice, the Sanchezes' granddaughter, enabled us to examine another kind of conversation, this one between two youth, both eager to learn how they can serve their communities. In proceeding through the account and in carrying out the exercises, we have seen that, in addition to a growing knowledge of the relevant subjects, certain spiritual qualities, attitudes and skills are required to sustain the conversations we are considering here.

In this and the next section of the unit we will explore themes of a different type—that is, those generally taken up for discussion during visits to families with youngsters participating in the educational programs promoted by the institute. As already indicated, teaching classes for children and guiding a junior youth group as an animator are acts of service addressed in subsequent courses, in Books 3 and 5 respectively. You may or may not be familiar with the corresponding two programs, depending on whether you took part in them yourself at an earlier age.

Let us look, first, at the content that often forms the basis for an ongoing conversation with the families of junior youth. We will imagine that some time has passed since we left our story and that Beatrice is now studying Book 2. Alejandra asks her friend if she would like to accompany her when she visits the families of several junior youth who are going to establish a group with her assistance. She eagerly accepts.

Alejandra explains to Beatrice what she envisions. "We will begin each visit," she informs her, "by introducing the parents to the program their son or daughter has shown an interest in joining and by mentioning that it is part of the community-building process moving forward in the neighborhood. We will then explore with them some of the concepts and ideas central to the program. This will be the first of a series of visits, and our hope is that, as the conversation advances over time, the family will not only actively support the group in a variety of ways but become the promoters of the spiritual empowerment of the junior youth in the community."

Alejandra and Beatrice go on to discuss some points they plan to raise with each family. They decide to write down all the ideas they think important, knowing they will cover only a few in the first visit and will address the rest in subsequent conversations. Here are the points they enumerate about the potentialities of junior youth:

- In the life of an individual, the three years between the ages of 12 and 15 are a crucial period—a stage of transition from childhood to maturity.

- We often refer to young people in this age range as "junior youth". They are no longer children but have not yet reached the fullness of youth.

- Unfortunately, there is an erroneous yet widely propagated image of junior youth as impulsive, rebellious, self-absorbed and prone to constant crisis. We, however, see them in a different light. It is true that, during this short period of life, we all experience rapid changes, physically, emotionally, and mentally. And it is also true that, as a result, we may show some rebelliousness. But, in reality, this is an age of great potential and of great promise.

- We ourselves were junior youth not so long ago and remember how we were affected by these changes. Sometimes we were courageous and sometimes timid. Sometimes we were quite sociable and other times very shy. We often expressed the desire to be left alone, while hoping to receive attention. We wanted to understand what things we were good at and what talents and abilities we have. And it mattered to us greatly how other people saw us and what they thought of our ideas.

- What is important to realize is that this kind of behavior is only temporary. In the life of a human being it is during these years that certain powers of the mind develop rapidly. We begin to seek answers to fundamental questions of existence. We analyze what goes on around us and question much of what we have been taught. And we are not as willing as we once were to follow automatically what adults tell us to do, especially when we see contradictions between their words and actions.

- If young people are to be assisted in applying fruitfully their emerging powers, it is essential to avoid treating them as children. Here is how 'Abdu'l-Bahá describes this period:

"After a time he enters the period of youth, in which his former conditions and needs are superseded by new requirements applicable to the advance in his degree. His faculties of observation are broadened and deepened; his intelligent capacities are trained and awakened; the limitations and environment of childhood no longer restrict his energies and accomplishments."[35]

- The Universal House of Justice, the governing body of the Bahá'í Faith, says this about the approach we have adopted in working with junior youth:

"While global trends project an image of this age group as problematic, lost in the throes of tumultuous physical and emotional change, unresponsive and self-consumed, the Bahá'í community—in the language it employs and the approaches it adopts—is moving decidedly in the opposite direction, seeing in junior youth instead altruism, an acute sense of justice, eagerness to learn about the universe and a desire to contribute to the construction of a better world."[36]

Alejandra and Beatrice next turn their attention to the spiritual empowerment program itself and try to identify some of its features:

- Those between the ages of 12 and 15 yearn to belong to a group of friends with whom they can share their thoughts, work on projects, play sports, and so on. For this reason, the program is built around the concept of a "junior youth group". Each group is guided by an "animator", often an older youth who, as a true friend to the members, assists them in developing their capacities.

- Groups meet regularly. In their meetings, junior youth learn to explore concepts and to express ideas with no fear of censor or ridicule. They are encouraged to listen, to speak, to reflect, to analyze, to make decisions, and to act on them.

- We live at a time when so many negative forces affect the way junior youth think and behave. Animators help them to combat these forces—not only to protect themselves from the moral decay of society but to work for the betterment of the world.

- The program seeks to nurture powers inherent in the human soul, powers that during early adolescence begin to manifest themselves in greater and greater degrees. Particularly important are the powers of thought and expression. Young people must develop the language needed both to express profound ideas about the world and to articulate how they want to see it change.

- Junior youth are eager to reflect on the meaning of concepts fundamental to a purposeful life. Happiness, hope, and excellence are a few examples. Regrettably people tend to talk about these ideas in superficial ways. Gaining a deep understanding of such concepts, recognizing how they find expression in everyday life, can assist young minds in building a sound moral structure and in withstanding the negative forces of society.

- Understanding concepts is essential to intellectual development. Junior youth can sometimes face difficulty at school because they are expected to learn a great deal of information on different subjects, without receiving sufficient help to grasp the underlying concepts. The program motivates them to think deeply about ideas—moral, mathematical, scientific, and so on—and this invariably improves their performance at school.

- Junior youth possess a great desire to make sense of things. They want to comprehend the reasons for what is happening around them. To succeed, they must be able to see not only with their physical eyes but also with the eye of the spirit. An important aim of the program, then, is the enhancement of spiritual perception: the ability to recognize spiritual forces and to identify spiritual principles in situations encountered.

- The program achieves its various aims—the development of morals, spiritual perception, and the powers of expression—with the aid of a series of texts. The texts consist of simple stories about the lives of young people in different parts of the world. Besides studying these texts together, discussing their content and completing the required exercises, the junior youth participate in sports and learn about arts and crafts.

- With the help of animators, groups also design and carry out a series of service projects, which is a major component of the program. Through these projects, junior youth learn to think about the community and its needs, to consult, and to collaborate among themselves and with others in the community.

- Subjects covered by the texts are varied; each focuses on a theme essential to the spiritual empowerment of junior youth. The first text, for example, treats the theme of "confirmation"—that God confirms the efforts we make to achieve noble goals. Another text is about "hope"—how we must look with hope towards the future even during the hardest of times. Another analyzes the concept of "excellence". "Joy" is the theme of one story, while "the power of the word" is the subject of reflection in another. Among the texts that address mathematical concepts, one explores the habits of an orderly mind. In the area of science, there is a text that focuses on taking care of one's health—physical, mental, and spiritual. And there are a dozen or so more that junior youth study during three years.

Alejandra and Beatrice plan to bring a couple of the texts with them, in case parents wish to glance through them. If you are not well acquainted with the texts, you may find it helpful to take some time to read as many of the stories as possible—this will enable you to better follow diverse conversations unfolding in the community. Meanwhile, you are encouraged to discuss fully with the other participants in your study group the ideas presented above, which are treated at greater depth in Book 5. If, after studying that book, you decide to act as an animator of a junior youth group, you will systematically visit the families of its members and explore with them these and many similar ideas. But even now, like Beatrice, you may wish to accompany someone with experience on a few visits to the families of junior youth in your community.

SECTION 15

The next day, Alejandra and Beatrice visit the homes of three junior youth who will be joining the new group being formed in the neighborhood. Beatrice is happy to see the enthusiasm with which the parents engage in conversation on the spiritual empowerment program. By the end of the afternoon, she is convinced that she would like to help Alejandra with the junior youth group and learn to serve as an animator of a new group herself, hopefully within the year. She realizes, of course, that she has a few institute books to complete in the meantime. But she is determined to advance in their study at the same steady pace that has gotten her this far.

So it is that, with constant assistance and encouragement from Alejandra, Beatrice moves forward on the path of service. Let us resume her story again, then, a few months later, when she is just about to finish Book 3. The tutor of her study circle has asked Maribel, a children's class teacher, to invite Beatrice and her fellow participants to accompany her, in turns, on visits to the parents of youngsters in a newly formed class for Grade 1. Beatrice feels she has learned a great deal from her study of Book 3. And she knows from Alejandra, who has mentioned it a few times, that the insights she has gained from the book will enhance her capacity to serve as an animator.

When they get together, Maribel tells Beatrice that they will be visiting the mother of Emma. "She is a delightful little girl who loves to learn," Maribel shares. "I have already visited her parents once and explained to them the nature of a Bahá'í children's class. They were happy to allow Emma to participate. Her mother expressed an interest in hearing more about the class, and I promised to go back and speak a little about the educational ideas underlying the material we teach. I have actually written some notes for myself. If you want, we can go through them together and talk about them." Beatrice agrees. Here are the notes they discuss:

- First, I will tell Mrs. Martinez how happy I am to have Emma in the class and will mention some of her wonderful qualities.

- It seems best to begin the discussion by reading with her this quotation from the Writings of Bahá'u'lláh:

"Regard man as a mine rich in gems of inestimable value. Education can, alone, cause it to reveal its treasures, and enable mankind to benefit therefrom."[37]

- I can then share a few thoughts about how much this statement has influenced me as a teacher. My heart overflows with joy, I will say, whenever I look at the children in the class and think of them as mines full of priceless gems. Every one of them has the potential to show forth heavenly qualities. Every one of them has talents that can be discovered and developed. Every one of them can grow up to become a valuable member of society and contribute to the betterment of the world.

- Next, I should probably give a few examples of the gems that education must strive to reveal in every child. I could mention some of the powers of the mind, say, to discover the laws of nature, to produce beautiful works of art, and to express noble thoughts. Children can begin to develop all these powers, I will explain, when they receive a proper education. But, for this to happen, they must acquire certain attributes at an early age. For example, they must learn to pay attention, to work hard when necessary, and to focus on what they are doing. They should grow into individuals who are concerned about the well-being of others and who want to serve the community. That is why it is important to attend to the development of their character at a young age.

- This will be a good place, then, to ask Mrs. Martinez to share with us a few ideas about the kind of person she wants her daughter to be. What are some of the character traits that she thinks are important for Emma to have?

- Among the attributes she mentions, some will, for sure, fall in the category of spiritual qualities, which is the next subject I will introduce. There are certain attributes an individual should possess, I will say, that are fundamental to human existence. They belong to the soul of the human being. We develop them as we polish the mirror of our heart so it can reflect the attributes of God. To these we refer as spiritual qualities, and the lessons we teach in our classes for Grade 1 focus mostly on these qualities.

- I think I will just go on and enumerate a few spiritual qualities addressed in the Grade 1 lessons in Book 3 and share with her the corresponding quotations. I will explain that Emma will memorize these quotations and that she could ask her daughter to recite them to her, as well as the prayers she will learn:

  - Love:

    "O Friend! In the garden of thy heart plant naught but the rose of love . . ."[38]

  - Justice:

    "Tread ye the path of justice, for this, verily, is the straight path."[39]

  - Truthfulness:

    "Truthfulness is the foundation of all human virtues."[40]

  - Joy:

    "O Son of Man! Rejoice in the gladness of thine heart, that thou mayest be worthy to meet Me and to mirror forth My beauty."[41]

Maribel and Beatrice decide that the above ideas are sufficient for one visit. You will soon move on to the study of Book 3 yourself and will have an opportunity to reflect on some principles that give shape to the Ruhi Institute's six-year program for the spiritual education of children. If, before then, the occasion arises for you to visit a few parents with a children's class teacher, the ideas set out here will prove to be of assistance, and you should discuss them now point by point in your study group.

SECTION 16

Earlier we read the following words of 'Abdu'l-Bahá: "The stronger the ties of fellowship and solidarity amongst men, the greater will be the power of constructiveness and accomplishment in all the planes of human activity." The Universal House of Justice tells us that, in paying visits to homes and in extending invitations to ours, we "are forging ties of spiritual kinship that foster a sense of community." We should not underestimate, then, the effect of this practice on the culture of our growing community.

In the preceding sections we have looked at several distinct kinds of conversation that can take place during the visits we make to one another's homes. All of us, as we walk the path of service, will participate in an expanding conversation in our village, town or neighborhood about the application of Bahá'u'lláh's teachings to our individual and collective lives. Sometimes this will unfold in a series of formal visits organized to enable increasing numbers to deepen their knowledge of these teachings. On numerous other occasions, the educational programs of the institute, their aims and content, will be the subject of discussion.

Invitations to engage in the community-building process will be extended to more and more neighbors and friends. As you look to the future, then, and to the path of service that stretches ahead of you, you should make every effort to learn the content presented in this unit well, gain experience conversing on each theme, and, of course, continue to deepen your own knowledge of Bahá'u'lláh's teachings. Thus will be yours the never-ending joy of sharing the Word of God with others.

REFERENCES

1. Bahá'u'lláh, *The Hidden Words* (Wilmette: Bahá'í Publishing Trust, 2003, 2012 printing), Arabic no. 4, p. 4.

2. Bahá'u'lláh, in *Bahá'í Prayers: A Selection of Prayers Revealed by Bahá'u'lláh, the Báb, and 'Abdu'l-Bahá* (Wilmette: Bahá'í Publishing Trust, 2002, 2017 printing), p. 4.

3. *Gleanings from the Writings of Bahá'u'lláh* (Wilmette: Bahá'í Publishing Trust, 1983, 2017 printing), IV, par. 1, p. 5.

4. Ibid., V, par. 2, pp. 6–7.

5. 'Abdu'l-Bahá, in *Bahá'í Prayers*, p. 81.

6. Ibid., p. 111.

7. Ibid.

8. From a talk given on 16 August 1912, published in *The Promulgation of Universal Peace: Talks Delivered by 'Abdu'l-Bahá during His Visit to the United States and Canada in 1912* (Wilmette: Bahá'í Publishing, 2012), par. 23, p. 364.

9. 'Abdu'l-Bahá, in *Bahá'í Prayers*, p. 130.

10. *Gleanings from the Writings of Bahá'u'lláh*, XLV, par. 1, pp. 111–12.

11. 'Abdu'l-Bahá, cited by Shoghi Effendi, *The World Order of Bahá'u'lláh: Selected Letters* (Wilmette: Bahá'í Publishing Trust, 1991, 2012 printing), p. 139.

12. *Gleanings from the Writings of Bahá'u'lláh*, V, par. 5, p. 8.

13. From a talk given by 'Abdu'l-Bahá on 5 May 1912, published in *The Promulgation of Universal Peace*, par. 4, p. 128.

14. From a talk given on 21 October 1911, published in *Paris Talks: Addresses Given by 'Abdu'l-Bahá in 1911* (Wilmette: Bahá'í Publishing, 2006, 2016 printing), no. 6.7–8, p. 22.

15. *Gleanings from the Writings of Bahá'u'lláh*, CXLVI, par. 1, p. 357.

16. From a talk given by 'Abdu'l-Bahá on 5 May 1912, published in *The Promulgation of Universal Peace*, par. 4, p. 128.

17. *The Hidden Words*, Persian no. 44, p. 37.

18. Ibid., Persian no. 66, p. 45.

19. From a Tablet of 'Abdu'l-Bahá. (authorized translation)

20. From a talk given by 'Abdu'l-Bahá on 25 September 1912, published in *The Promulgation of Universal Peace*, par. 2, pp. 478–79.

21. *Selections from the Writings of 'Abdu'l-Bahá* (Wilmette: Bahá'í Publishing, 2010, 2015 printing), no. 43.1, p. 125.

22. Ibid., no. 207.3, p. 360.

23. Bahá'u'lláh, in *Bahá'í Meetings: Extracts from the Writings of Bahá'u'lláh, 'Abdu'l-Bahá, and Shoghi Effendi*, compiled by the Research Department of the Universal House of Justice (Wilmette: Bahá'í Publishing Trust, 1976, 1980 printing), p. 3.

24. Ibid.

25. *Tablets of Abdul-Baha Abbas* (New York: Bahá'í Publishing Committee, 1916, 1930 printing), vol. 3, p. 631. (authorized translation)

26. Bahá'u'lláh, in *The Kitáb-i-Aqdas: The Most Holy Book* (Wilmette: Bahá'í Publishing Trust, 1993, 2013 printing), par. 57, p. 41.

27. *Selections from the Writings of 'Abdu'l-Bahá*, no. 48.1, p. 130.

28. From a letter dated 27 August 1989, published in *Messages from the Universal House of Justice, 1986–2001: The Fourth Epoch of the Formative Age* (Wilmette: Bahá'í Publishing Trust, 2010), no. 69.2, pp. 132–33.

29. Ibid., no. 69.9–10, p. 135.

30. *The Hidden Words*, Persian no. 82, p. 51.

31. Ibid., Persian no. 80, p. 51.

32. 'Abdu'l-Bahá, *The Secret of Divine Civilization* (Wilmette: Bahá'í Publishing, 2007, 2016 printing), par. 46, p. 33.

33. *The Hidden Words*, Persian no. 49, p. 39.

34. Shoghi Effendi, cited in *Bahá'í News*, no. 13 (September 1926), p. 1.

35. From a talk given by 'Abdu'l-Bahá on 17 November 1912, published in *The Promulgation of Universal Peace*, par. 3, p. 617.

36. From a message dated 21 April 2010, published in *Framework for Action: Selected Messages of the Universal House of Justice and Supplementary Material, 2006–2016* (West Palm Beach: Palabra Publications, 2017), no. 14.16, p. 82.

37. *Gleanings from the Writings of Bahá'u'lláh*, CXXII, par. 1, p. 294.

38. *The Hidden Words*, Persian no. 3, p. 23.

39.   *Gleanings from the Writings of Bahá'u'lláh*, CXVIII, par. 1, p. 283.

40.   'Abdu'l-Bahá, cited by Shoghi Effendi, *The Advent of Divine Justice* (Wilmette: Bahá'í Publishing Trust, 2006, 2018 printing), par. 40, p. 39.

41.   *The Hidden Words*, Arabic no. 36, p. 12.